Should the Drinking Age Be Lowered?

Hal Marcovitz

INCONTROVERSY

ReferencePoint
Press®

San Diego, CA

For more information, contact:
ReferencePoint Press, Inc.
PO Box 27779
San Diego, CA 92198
www.ReferencePointPress.com

LIBRARY OF CONGRESS CATALOGING-IN-PUBLICATION DATA

Marcovitz, Hal.
  Should the drinking age be lowered? / by Hal Marcovitz.
    p. cm. -- (In controversy)
  Includes bibliographical references and index.
  ISBN-13: 978-1-60152-144-6 (hardback)
  ISBN-10: 1-60152-144-8 (hardback)
  1. Teenagers--Alcohol use. 2. Drinking age. 3. Drinking age--Law and legislation--United States. I. Title.
  HV5135.M357 2011
  362.292'6--dc22
                                                              2010026450

Contents

Foreword

In 2008, as the U.S. economy and economies worldwide were falling into the worst recession since the Great Depression, most Americans had difficulty comprehending the complexity, magnitude, and scope of what was happening. As is often the case with a complex, controversial issue such as this historic global economic recession, looking at the problem as a whole can be overwhelming and often does not lead to understanding. One way to better comprehend such a large issue or event is to break it into smaller parts. The intricacies of global economic recession may be difficult to understand, but one can gain insight by instead beginning with an individual contributing factor such as the real estate market. When examined through a narrower lens, complex issues become clearer and easier to evaluate.

This is the idea behind ReferencePoint Press's *In Controversy* series. The series examines the complex, controversial issues of the day by breaking them into smaller pieces. Rather than looking at the stem cell research debate as a whole, a title would examine an important aspect of the debate such as *Is Stem Cell Research Necessary?* or *Is Embryonic Stem Cell Research Ethical?* By studying the central issues of the debate individually, researchers gain a more solid and focused understanding of the topic as a whole.

Each book in the series provides a clear, insightful discussion of the issues, integrating facts and a variety of contrasting opinions for a solid, balanced perspective. Personal accounts and direct quotes from academic and professional experts, advocacy groups, politicians, and others enhance the narrative. Sidebars add depth to the discussion by expanding on important ideas and events. For quick reference, a list of key facts concludes every chapter. Source notes, an annotated organizations list, bibliography, and index provide student researchers with additional tools for papers and class discussion.

The *In Controversy* series also challenges students to think critically about issues, to improve their problem-solving skills, and to sharpen their ability to form educated opinions. As President Barack Obama stated in a March 2009 speech, success in the twenty-first century will not be measurable merely by students' ability to "fill in a bubble on a test but whether they possess 21st century skills like problem-solving and critical thinking and entrepreneurship and creativity." Those who possess these skills will have a strong foundation for whatever lies ahead.

No one can know for certain what sort of world awaits today's students. What we can assume, however, is that those who are inquisitive about a wide range of issues; open-minded to divergent views; aware of bias and opinion; and able to reason, reflect, and reconsider will be best prepared for the future. As the international development organization Oxfam notes, "Today's young people will grow up to be the citizens of the future: but what that future holds for them is uncertain. We can be quite confident, however, that they will be faced with decisions about a wide range of issues on which people have differing, contradictory views. If they are to develop as global citizens all young people should have the opportunity to engage with these controversial issues."

In Controversy helps today's students better prepare for tomorrow. An understanding of the complex issues that drive our world and the ability to think critically about them are essential components of contributing, competing, and succeeding in the twenty-first century.

Reopening the Debate

At Washington and Lee University in Lexington, Virginia, school officials have been vigilant in banning drinking on campus. Students are expected to abide by Virginia law, which prohibits drinking by anybody under the age of 21. In addition to facing criminal prosecution by state authorities, Washington and Lee students found to be drinking on campus face harsh measures by the university: They could be suspended for a semester and, if they are repeat offenders, expelled from school.

However, university officials are also well aware of a major consequence of the school's alcohol ban: By clamping down on drinking on campus, they have helped drive drinking *off* campus. Therefore, on weekend nights, it is not unusual to find students drinking at parties just a few blocks away in off-campus housing, where many Washington and Lee students live. "It's a funny situation we've created with this drinking age," says Kenneth Ruscio, Washington and Lee president. "It could be driving behavior farther and farther away and making it more and more difficult to respond to irresponsible drinking. Students drink more than they should. They drink in ways that aren't really responsible."[1]

One of the ways in which university officials have responded is to make a free shuttle bus available to ferry students home from off-campus parties, mostly to discourage intoxicated students from driving back to school. The bus makes its rounds through nearby neighborhoods, but students can even call for the bus when they are ready to go home. Student Katie Dunphy says the shuttle is a very popular feature of university life—at times, she says, students have broken into song while riding home from parties. "All of the students love it," she says. "It can be pretty fun."[2]

Dim View of Teenage Drinking

At Washington and Lee, the existence of a free shuttle bus for intoxicated students illustrates the position in which many universities find themselves. They have banned drinking on campus, yet they acknowledge that despite their rules, young people will find places to drink and abuse alcoholic beverages. By banning alcohol on campus, universities are essentially upholding underage drinking laws that have been adopted by all state legislatures starting in the mid-1970s. At the time, the legal drinking age in many states was 18 or 19, but then state lawmakers as well as federal authorities started taking a dim view of teenage drinking, finding that most young people do not know how to drink responsibly and very often endanger themselves and others by driving while intoxicated. According to the National Highway Traffic Safety Administration, nearly 25,000 lives have been saved since 1974, when state governments started raising the minimum age for legal drinking to 21.

While such statistics might suggest the argument about lowering the drinking age is closed, that is not necessarily the case. Many university officials acknowledge that alcohol abuse, particularly binge drinking, is a growing problem among college students as well as younger people. A binge drinker is defined as a male who consumes at least five drinks during a single drinking occasion and a female who consumes at least four drinks.

"Students drink more than they should. They drink in ways that aren't really responsible."[1]

— Washington and Lee University president Kenneth Ruscio.

These university officials have launched a movement known as the Amethyst Initiative to reconsider the nation's drinking age laws, with an eye toward lowering the legal drinking age to 18 or 19. (An amethyst is a purple gemstone believed by the ancient Greeks to be an antidote for intoxication.) "The law is out of step with reality,"[3] says John McCardell, a history professor and former president of Middlebury College in Vermont.

McCardell and officials at other American colleges contend that if students could drink legally, they would be less prone to

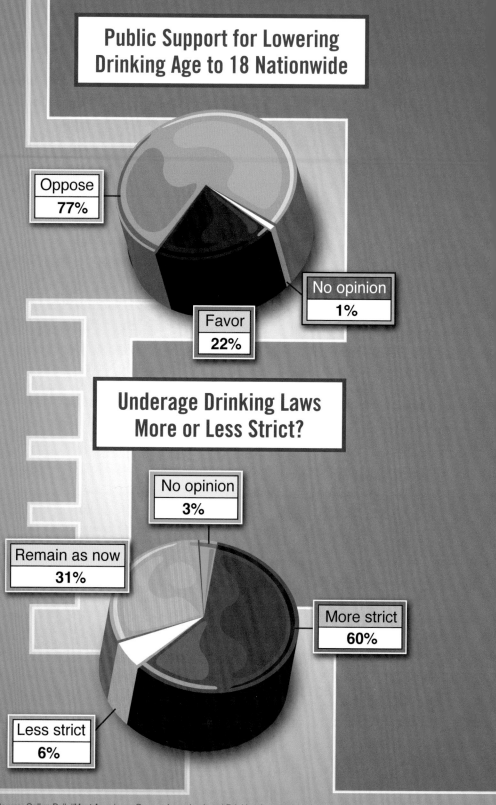

Public Support for Lowering Drinking Age to 18 Nationwide

Oppose
77%

No opinion
1%

Favor
22%

Underage Drinking Laws More or Less Strict?

No opinion
3%

Remain as now
31%

More strict
60%

Less strict
6%

Source: Gallup Poll, "Most Americans Oppose Lowering Legal Drinking Age to 18 Nationwide," July 27, 2007. www.gallup.com.

A large majority of Americans, 77 percent, say they would oppose a federal law to lower the drinking age in all states to 18, according to a 2007 Gallup poll. Additionally, the poll found that 60 percent of Americans believe the penalties for underage drinking should be strengthened. Pollsters say these views have changed little when compared with poll results from the 6 years prior to the survey.

abuse alcohol. Indeed, they suggest that if a student started drinking to excess in a bar, the bartender could refuse to serve him or her and that the student would probably be asked to leave the premises. With students drinking in secret, though, McCardell argues that there is no one in authority to turn off the tap, meaning young drinkers continue to consume alcohol in dangerously high amounts. "There's a public interest in reopening this debate,"[4] insists McCardell.

Alcohol-Related Deaths

One of the signers of the Amethyst Initiative, Washington and Lee's Ruscio, has recognized that despite his school's crackdown on drinking, alcohol abuse remains a major problem among students. Establishing the shuttle bus is one of the steps taken by school officials to help reduce the dangers of drinking at Washington and Lee. Among the others are offering counseling to students who are recognized as alcohol abusers and establishing a probationary program in which students must remain alcohol-free for a year or risk expulsion.

University officials toughened the school's drinking policies following five alcohol-related deaths during the 1990s. In one case an intoxicated student fell to his death out of a dormitory window. In another case two students, junior Adam Burchett and freshman Kristin Shelton, died when their car, driven by Burchett, struck two trees near Burchett's off-campus apartment. The car flipped over several times before landing in a ditch. According to state police, both students visited several parties in the hours leading up to the accident, and both students were intoxicated. "[The Burchett incident] was the straw that broke the camel's back,"[5] says Dawn Watkins, dean of student affairs at Washington and Lee.

Since the bus started making its runs in 2000, there have been no alcohol-related deaths involving Washington and Lee students. Despite the success of the shuttle bus, though, Washington and Lee officials know that students will continue to drink, and there is little they can do if some of those intoxicated students decide that rather than taking the bus, they will risk driving themselves home instead.

Facts

- According to the National Highway Traffic Safety Administration, about 28 percent of drivers between the ages of 15 and 20 who are killed in car accidents were drinking shortly before their deaths.

- College students between the ages of 18 and 22 are more likely to be drinkers than people in that age group who do not attend college, according to the Substance Abuse and Mental Health Services Administration.

CHAPTER ONE

What Are the Origins of the Drinking Age Controversy?

According to a study by the National Highway Traffic Safety Administration, there is a clear connection between young people and alcohol abuse. The study found that 25 percent of eighth-grade students, 40 percent of tenth-grade students, and 53 percent of high school seniors have consumed alcohol. "Not only is drinking a prevalent problem among youth, but many of those who drink also drive after drinking," reports the study. "Fifteen percent of students in grades 9–12 (ages 15–18) surveyed . . . reported driving after drinking during the month before being surveyed, and more than one-third reported riding with a driver who had been drinking."[6] Adds Chuck Hurley, executive director of the advocacy group Mothers Against Drunk Driving (MADD): "The inconvenient truth is that a drinking age at 18 would cause more funerals. Nine hundred families a year would have to bury a teenager."[7]

Such statistics, as well as the accompanying rhetoric by experts such as Hurley, illustrate the seriousness with which government regulators and others regard the issue of underage drinking. Over the course of American history, that has not always been the case. Indeed, for many years alcohol abuse by young people was not regarded as a widespread problem, mostly because alcohol abuse by adults was also not considered a problem of significant consequences. "Drunkards usually were locked into the judicial system, with regular topers [excessive drinkers] arrested over and over again but provided with no medical or psychological treatment," write historians Mark Edward Lender and James Kirby Martin. "Ambivalent and pre-occupied . . . America lacked programs either to prevent problem drinking or to assist the problem drinker—even after the medical ill effects of alcoholism had been well documented."[8] In fact, it has only been since the 1980s that lawmakers elevated the offense of driving while intoxicated to the status of a crime punishable by jail.

Over the years, the regulation of who could drink, and at what age they could start drinking, was largely left up to state governments, which responded by passing laws of varying degrees that often worked in conflict with one another. For example, for decades the minimum drinking age in Pennsylvania was 21, but in New Jersey, New York, and Ohio, states that border Pennsylvania, the legal drinking age was 18. This meant that an 18-year-old

A Vermont state trooper inspects a car involved in an accident that killed four teenagers. The four were returning from a night of drinking in Quebec, Canada, where the drinking age is 18. The drinking age in Vermont is 21.

from Pennsylvania could borrow the keys to the family car and, after making a brief drive, find numerous places in a neighboring state willing to sell him or her liquor. The drive back across the state line was often performed by a young driver attempting to negotiate the tricky roads home after a night of drinking—frequently with tragic results.

Early Views of Alcohol

Alcohol use dates back thousands of years—archaeologists have uncovered evidence that indicates people were fermenting beverages as far back as 10,000 B.C. and that people may have learned how to make beer before they learned how to make bread. According to the Old Testament, when the waters of the Great Flood receded and Noah arrived at Mount Ararat, one of his first chores was to plant a vineyard.

When the first colonists arrived in Virginia in the 1600s, beer made the trip along with them. Even the Puritans appreciated a good drink—although they preached moderation. "Drink is in itself a good creature of God, and to be received with thankfulness," said the Puritan minister Increase Mather, "but the abuse of drink is from Satan; the wine is from God, but the drunkard is from the devil."[9] Later, Thomas Jefferson is known to have drafted the Declaration of Independence with an open bottle of wine on his desk. Indeed, drinking became such an important part of the fabric of American society that in 1794, a tax on whiskey sparked a rebellion in which some 500 farmers in western Pennsylvania took up arms against government tax collectors. The uprising, known as the Whiskey Rebellion, was crushed when President Washington sent in federal troops.

Starting in the early 1800s, states regulated the sale of alcohol, but these laws were intended mostly to crack down on public drunkenness rather than making sure alcohol was kept out of the hands of minors. During the early history of America, the prevailing attitude was that alcohol helped improve health—that a shot or two of whiskey a day did the body good. "Scarcely any age [was] deemed exempt from its application," write Lender and Martin. "Even school children took their sip of whiskey, the morning and

How Much Is Too Much?

All states have adopted the standard of a blood alcohol content (BAC) of 0.08—8/100 of 1 percent—as evidence that a driver is impaired. However, some people seem to be able to drink for hours without suffering from a loss of coordination or alertness. Others get tipsy after a single drink. The reasons for this difference depend a lot on the gender and weight of the drinker as well as other issues, such as how quickly the drinks are consumed and whether the drinker has a full stomach (alcohol is absorbed more slowly after a meal).

Many state and local law enforcement authorities have published charts indicating how alcohol may affect people. The chart published by the campus police at the University of Oklahoma suggests that a male who weighs 170 pounds (77kg) and consumes 4 drinks within an hour will register a BAC of 0.08 and will, therefore, be legally drunk. Likewise, the Oklahoma chart reports, a female who weighs 137 pounds (62kg) and consumes 3 drinks in an hour will register a BAC of 0.08. The Oklahoma chart identifies a drink as a cocktail that includes 1.25 ounces (37.5ml) of liquor, a 12-ounce (355ml) beer, or a 4-ounce (120ml) glass of wine.

afternoon glasses being considered absolute indispensable to man and boy."[10]

By and large, Americans chose to leave it up to families, rather than elected officials, to decide at what age it was acceptable to start drinking. Also, alcohol could be expensive—few farm boys were likely able to scrape together the 10 cents they may have needed to buy a mug of ale at the town saloon. Says legal historian Carla T. Main, "The expense and limited availability of liquor . . . helped keep it out of youthful hands."[11]

The Arrival of Prohibition

Nevertheless, many leaders of early American society looked on the drinking habits of Americans with a growing sense of horror, giving rise to an influential temperance movement. By the second half of the nineteenth century, industrialization had swept through the country; cities became crowded and crime flourished. Temperance leaders blamed alcohol for crime, the stresses on families, and other ills of society.

In 1918 temperance advocates won passage of the law they had sought for decades: an amendment to the U.S. Constitution banning all alcohol consumption in America. The Eighteenth Amendment took effect in 1920. A separate law, known as the National Prohibition Act, was adopted by Congress to provide the federal government with the authority to determine exactly what constituted an alcoholic beverage (according to the act, any beverage containing at least one-half of 1 percent alcohol qualified as an intoxicating drink.) The act also empowered federal agents to enforce the law.

The National Prohibition Act is more commonly known as the Volstead Act, named for its prime sponsor, Andrew J. Volstead, a member of Congress from Minnesota. If Volstead and other anti-drinking advocates failed to realize at the time just how unpopular this new law would turn out to be, they would find out in the 1922 election. In that election the alcohol-deprived voters of Minnesota rewarded their congressman for sponsoring the National Prohibition Act by booting him out of office.

A Right of Citizenship

During the era known as Prohibition, millions of Americans routinely ignored the law, while powerful criminal syndicates of bootleggers and rum runners supplied beer and liquor to thirsty customers. At the height of Prohibition, it was estimated that there were some 200,000 speakeasies—illegal bars and nightclubs—operating in America. Finally, after 13 years of trying in vain to enforce a largely unenforceable law, exasperated lawmakers voted to repeal the Eighteenth Amendment.

Following Prohibition, the states returned to regulating alcohol sales and consumption. Within a few years they had ad-

During Prohibition, millions of Americans illicitly sold or drank alcohol in defiance of the 13-year ban on alcohol consumption. In this 1931 photograph, a woman shows off a vest and pant-apron designed for hiding alcohol while crossing the border.

opted a smorgasbord of laws decreeing who could drink, who could sell alcoholic beverages, and when and where drinking could occur. Some states remained "dry" for several years—the last holdout, Oklahoma, finally permitted alcohol sales in 1959. (Even today municipal ordinances remain on the books of many towns and townships across the United States, banning liquor sales within their borders.) Some states, such as Mississippi, enacted partial bans—beer and wine sales were legalized, but distilled spirits were banned (legislators finally lifted the ban in the

1960s). Some states, such as Pennsylvania, went into the liquor business, establishing a system of "state stores" that sell bottled liquors and wines while banning private sales of those beverages except by the glass in licensed bars. Pennsylvania lawmakers have maintained the state store system into the twenty-first century; only beer is available through private vendors—and not in supermarkets or convenience stores, but in licensed beer distributorships only.

The states also adopted their own legal drinking ages. In the years following the repeal of Prohibition, 32 states adopted minimum legal drinking ages of 21. At the time, the national voting age was 21, and many state lawmakers considered the voting age to be the age at which rights of citizenship are granted—the so-called age of majority. Evidently, one of those rights of citizenship included the right to drink.

However, some state lawmakers with more liberal mindsets disagreed. Following Prohibition, 16 states set their minimum drinking ages at 18 to 20. Still, even in progressive states like New York, which set its minimum legal drinking age at 18, there remained vocal opposition to teenagers drinking. In the fall of 1939, while addressing students at Colgate University in Hamilton, New York, school president George Barton Cutten had this to say about drinking: "We have been hearing considerable lately about teaching young men to drink like gentlemen—whatever that means. I can speak for college students and say that I have rarely seen them act otherwise than as gentlemen except when they were drinking."[12]

Political Upheaval

Meanwhile, educators in high schools were not sure what to teach their students about drinking. After all, from 1920 through 1933, drinking had been outlawed. During Prohibition the message delivered in classrooms was simple: Do not drink, because it is against the law. Now, with drinking once again legal, educators were at a loss as to what to tell students about alcohol. In essence, no one had a lesson plan that covered what constituted alcohol abuse. Historians Lender and Martin write: "In the absence of temperance instruction manuals, no one had

"I can speak for college students and say that I have rarely seen them act otherwise than as gentlemen except when they were drinking."[12]

— Colgate University president George Barton Cutten.

alternatives to offer. . . . [It was not] that educators endorsed drink but they lacked a clear idea of what to do with the subject."[13]

These varieties of laws and attitudes about drinking remained in place into the 1960s, but with the implementation of the military draft during the Vietnam War era, many states agreed to look again at their drinking laws. By law, young men were required to register for the draft at the age of 18. Draftees questioned why they were old enough to risk their lives in the service of their country yet not old enough to enjoy a beer while on leave. One Vietnam War veteran, William D. Ehrhart, recalls arriving home after his year of combat in Southeast Asia and discovering, at the age of 19, that he was still too young to drink legally in his hometown of Perkasie, Pennsylvania. So he joined the local Veterans of Foreign Wars (VFW) post, not because he felt an affinity for the VFW, but because he knew the bartender at the post would serve him a drink. "I knew that the local VFW had a bar where the only card the bartender asked to see was your VFW membership card, so I figured that it would be a place where I could drink without getting hassled,"[14] he says.

Ehrhart arrived home from Vietnam in 1969. Not only was he not old enough to drink legally, but he also was not old enough to vote. Indeed, the same arguments that draftees were making about the legal drinking age were being made with regard to the voting age, which at the time was 21. Congress responded to these complaints—it did seem unfair that 18-year-olds were prohibited by law from casting votes for or against political leaders who had the power to send them off to war. In 1972 the Twenty-sixth Amendment to the Constitution took effect, giving 18-year-old citizens the right to vote. As for the drinking age, by the early 1970s, 29 states had lowered their legal drinking ages to 18 or 19. Says Main, "The legal drinking age got swept up in the political upheaval of the era, as states generally reexamined their age-of-majority laws."[15]

Alcohol Is a Drug

The trend started reversing in the mid-1970s. By then the draft had ended, but many of those laws permitting teenag-

> "I knew that the local VFW had a bar where the only card the bartender asked to see was your VFW membership card, so I figured that it would be a place where I could drink without getting hassled."[14]
>
> —Nineteen-year-old Vietnam War veteran William D. Ehrhart.

ers to drink remained on the books. And by then, statistics started piling up indicating that younger drinkers were more likely to abuse alcohol, particularly behind the wheel. For example, statistics showed that although teenagers made up just 7 percent of licensed drivers in America, they were involved in 15 percent of all alcohol-related fatal accidents. Proponents of raising the legal drinking age to 21 cited studies that said as many as 5,000 lives a year could be saved by making it illegal for people under 21 to drink. "When the United States reduced its drinking age in the Seventies it was a public health disaster," says Hurley, the MADD executive director. "Death rates in the states that reduced their drinking age jumped 10 to 40 percent."[16]

"The legal drinking age got swept up in the political upheaval of the era, as states generally re-examined their age-of-majority laws."[15]

—Carla T. Main, legal historian.

Alcohol was also being reclassified as something other than a form of nourishment. In the late 1970s the National Institute on Alcohol Abuse and Alcoholism declared alcohol a drug and found that it was the most widely abused drug in American society. The problems of alcoholism could no longer be ignored. Instead of just tossing the drinker into the drunk tank for the night, where he or she could sleep it off, rehabilitative programs were offered to alcohol abusers.

Not only was alcohol now classified as a drug, but it had emerged as the drug of choice for young people. A study by the National Institute on Drug Abuse found that alcohol was the first drug that teenagers used, and it was likely to be the drug most teenagers tended to use over and over again. In 1981 it was estimated that there were 12 million alcohol abusers in America, and 3 million of them were teenagers.

Public opinion was clearly turning against alcohol abuse in all its forms. In 1980 the 13-year-old daughter of Candace Lightner was killed by a drunken driver who, it turned out, was a repeat offender. Prior to the accident that took the life of Lightner's daughter Cari, the man had been arrested for drunken driving four times. Lightner was appalled to find out that state laws did not regard drunken driving as a serious crime—offenders were often let off with fines or light sentences that may not have included

The Birth of MADD

Mothers Against Drunk Driving (MADD) was born shortly after May 13, 1980, when a car driven by Clarence Busch, 46, slammed into 13-year-old Cari Lightner as the teenager walked along a street in Sacramento, California. The impact was so severe that the girl's body was propelled more than 120 feet (36.6m) through the air. She died of massive internal injuries.

When Cari's mother, Candace Lightner, learned Busch had been drunk, she demanded to see his driving records. Clerks at the California Department of Motor Vehicles refused. She was also turned down by judges and state legislators.

Lightner felt that the victims of drunken driving deserved more than to be stonewalled, so she founded MADD to lobby for victims' rights as well as tough drunken driving laws. The movement soon spread to other cities. In Milwaukee, Wisconsin, 80 people showed up at the first meeting of the city's MADD chapter. "I sat there and said, 'What do I do now with all these people who want to volunteer?'" said Mickey Sadoff, who organized the Milwaukee chapter. "So we started to go to court with families to monitor drunk driving cases."

Busch served two and a half years in prison after his conviction in the death of Cari Lightner. Five years later, he was arrested for drunken driving again and was sentenced to four years in prison.

Quoted in *Driven*, "25 Years of Saving Lives," Fall 2005, p. 11. www.madd.org.

jail time. "Alcoholism may be a disease, but drunk driving is a crime,"[17] Lightner said shortly after the arrest of the driver who killed her daughter.

Lightner would go on to found MADD, launching a national campaign to make driving under the influence a serious offense.

Within a few years of MADD's founding, all states would adopt stiff, no-nonsense laws to crack down on driving under the influence. Typically, offenders face penalties that include steep fines, loss of their licenses, mandatory counseling, community service, and jail time.

Crossing State Lines

Given the statistics that were accumulating linking young people with alcohol abuse, as well as the efforts by groups like MADD to criminalize drinking and driving, many state legislatures responded by raising their states' minimum drinking ages. Their efforts were supported at the federal level; in 1983 a commission established by President Ronald Reagan to study the nation's drinking laws recommended that all states raise their minimum drinking ages to 21. "Studies have shown that raising the legal drinking age produced an average annual reduction of 28 percent in nighttime fatal crashes involving affected 18- to 21-year-old drivers,"[18] reported the commission.

"Alcoholism may be a disease, but drunk driving is a crime." [17]

— Candace Lightner, founder of Mothers Against Drunk Driving.

The commission was particularly concerned about what would happen if some states established minimum legal drinking ages at 21 while others kept lower drinking ages in place. The commission envisioned teenagers driving across state lines to binge, then racing back home intoxicated. Concluded the commission, "There is simply no way to adequately address the needless tragedies caused by young persons commuting to border states except by establishing a uniform drinking age among the states."[19] Added James J. Florio, a member of Congress from New Jersey who favored a national minimum drinking age of 21: "Teenagers drive across state borders to find a low legal drinking age and kill themselves on the way back. . . . The highway carnage is an interstate and national problem that requires national action."[20]

A year after the commission issued its report, Congress adopted the Uniform Drinking Age Act. The act did not set a national minimum legal drinking age but penalized any state that permitted drinking below the age of 21 by withholding 10 percent of the state's federal highway funds. Since states rely heavily on the billions of dollars a year they receive from the federal government to help them build and repair roads, most states that had not raised their minimum legal drinking ages by then quickly brought their laws into compliance with the federal act. The last state to raise its legal drinking age to 21 was Louisiana, which delayed implementation of the law until 1995. In Louisiana the economy of the state's largest city, New Orleans, relies heavily on the party atmosphere of the city's French Quarter, and state lawmakers were loathe to deny business to the numerous bars in the quarter. Nevertheless, Louisiana finally complied, and now, with very few exceptions, it is illegal everywhere in America for somebody under the age of 21 to consume alcoholic beverages.

A National Standard

In the years since the states raised their minimum legal drinking ages to 21, the crackdown on drunken driving has continued. Most of those efforts have focused on developing a national standard for what constitutes driving under the influence.

When a police officer stops a suspected intoxicated driver, in most cases the officer will administer what is known as the field sobriety test. This is a test performed along the road in which the officer will ask the driver to perform a number of relatively simple acts, such as walking in a straight line, standing on one leg, reciting the alphabet, counting backward, or touching the nose with eyes closed. By observing the suspect performing these tasks, the officer can make a preliminary judgment about whether the driver may have been drinking.

The next step, which is typically performed at the police station, is the administration of a breath test. The driver will be asked to blow into a machine known as a Breathalyzer, which can analyze, through air exhaled by the lungs, the alcohol content of the suspect's blood. Alcohol is absorbed into the blood through the stomach; the blood then circulates through the alveoli, which are the tiny air sacs in the lungs. When the driver exhales into the tube, the driver is actually exhaling tiny particles of alcohol that have accumulated in the air sacs. From an analysis of these tiny

"Teenagers drive across state borders to find a low legal drinking age and kill themselves on the way back. . . . The highway carnage is an interstate and national problem that requires national action."[20]

— James J. Florio, member of Congress from New Jersey who favored a national minimum drinking age of 21.

particles, the machine can determine what is known as the blood alcohol content, or BAC.

The Blood Alcohol Test

For several years many states recognized a BAC of 0.10—or one-tenth of 1 percent—as the threshold for legal intoxication. The results of Breathalyzer tests are used in court by prosecutors, who are required to prove a BAC level that meets the state's legal definition of intoxication in order to win convictions against defendants.

Many states recognized lower BACs as the threshold for intoxication. Efforts by MADD and similar advocacy groups to adopt a national BAC standard were rewarded in 2000 when Congress established 0.08, or 8/100 of 1 percent, as the nationally recognized threshold to determine legal intoxication. As with the minimum legal drinking age, Congress tied the availability of highway funds to the adoption of a BAC of 0.08, and within a short time all state governments complied.

Today the national attitude facing young people who drink is far different than the attitude they may have faced a century

A driver undergoes a field sobriety test in Minnesota. The test is given to drivers who are suspected of being intoxicated. During such a test, a police officer might ask a driver to walk in a straight line, stand on one foot, or perform other simple tasks.

ago. Instead of the notion that drinking is simply a healthy part of living, alcohol abuse is recognized as a disease. Moreover, underage drinking—and in addition, drinking and driving—is now regarded as a serious offense. Yet statistics continue to show that many young people are more than willing to defy the law.

Facts

- According to the FBI, in 1979, after many states had lowered their legal drinking ages, nearly 191,000 people under the age of 21 were arrested for driving while intoxicated. In 1967, a year in which most states maintained a minimum legal drinking age of 21, fewer than 18,000 people under 21 were arrested for drunken driving.

- Statistics compiled by Mothers Against Drunk Driving suggest that a person with a blood alcohol content of 0.08 is 16 times more likely to be involved in a car crash than somebody who has not consumed alcohol.

- A 1983 poll conducted by the Gallup Organization found that 77 percent of Americans favored a national minimum legal drinking age of 21.

- A 1978 study by the National Institute on Alcohol Abuse and Alcoholism reported that 80 percent of high school students reported drinking at least once a month. The study also said that 31 percent of the students admitted to getting drunk at least 6 times a year.

- A study conducted by the Pacific Institute for Research and Evaluation, which explores the impact of substance abuse, found that nearly half the teenagers arrested in alcohol-related accidents have blood alcohol levels of only 0.02 percent—normally a level produced by less than a single drink.

Are Teenagers Mature Enough to Drink?

Opponents of lowering the drinking age to 18 point to the sad case of Gordie Bailey as proof that nobody that young should be allowed anywhere near an alcoholic beverage. Bailey, 18 years old, had just enrolled in the University of Colorado when he attended a fraternity initiation. The older fraternity members led the pledges into the woods, where they built a campfire and rolled out 10 gallon-sized bottles (3.8L) of hard liquor and wine. They told the 26 pledges that to gain membership in the fraternity, they would have to consume the entire supply.

Bailey did his share to drain the bottles. Later, it was estimated that he consumed as much as 20 ounces (567g) of hard liquor. (The typical cocktail contains a single ounce or so of liquor). Soon after the initiation rite ended, Bailey's friends noticed something terribly wrong. "His eyes were rolling back in his head and he couldn't walk," Bailey's stepfather, Michael Lanahan, said later. "This wasn't somebody who just had too much to drink. He was clearly in trauma."[21]

Back at the fraternity house, Bailey passed out on the sofa. The next morning, when the fraternity members were unable to rouse him, they called for help. When the paramedics arrived, they were also unable to revive the boy. In fact, Bailey had died overnight, a victim of alcohol poisoning. He had consumed so much alcohol in such a short time that his breathing slowed and his heart shut down.

While there is no question that the events surrounding Bailey's death are truly tragic, the fact is, Bailey's case is not an isolated incident. According to the National Institute on Alcohol Abuse and Alcoholism, some 1,400 college students die each year of alcohol-related causes.

The fraternity party initiation that proved lethal in Bailey's case shows that many young drinkers do not consume alcohol the way most adults drink. In fact, the vast majority of America's 217 million people over 21 drink in moderation: a cocktail after work with friends, a martini at lunch to help close a business deal, a glass of wine in a restaurant with dinner, and a beer or two at the baseball game are all typical ways in which adults enjoy alcoholic beverages. For many young people, though, drinking is considered a game and hardly done in moderation.

Beer Hunter, Beer Pong, and the Century Club

In fact, there are dozens of drinking games. One popular game among young drinkers is Beer Hunter—everybody opens their beer bottles at the same time; the unlucky loser opens the bottle that has been pre-shaken, getting a shot of suds in the face. While the loser wipes off his or her face, the winners drain their bottles. After several rounds of Beer Hunter, it is likely that most of the players are too drunk to be terribly bothered when they lose.

There is also Beer Pong. The rules of the game are simple: Cups of beer are placed at either end of a Ping-Pong table. Competitors try to knock balls into the cups. When one lands in a cup, the player at that end of the table must drain the cup. The game ends when all the cups are drained or, more likely, when the players are too drunk to continue.

And then there is Century Club: All players must drink 1 ounce (29.5ml) of beer every minute for 100 straight minutes. Since a typical beer can contains 12 ounces (354ml), to successfully join the Century Club the player must consume the equivalent of more than 5 cans within an hour. *If* the player is able to finish, such a massive amount of alcohol consumed in such a short period of time would result in a blood alcohol content level of 0.17 in a 170-pound (77kg) male

"His eyes were rolling back in his head and he couldn't walk. This wasn't somebody who just had too much to drink. He was clearly in trauma."[21]

— Michael Lanahan, stepfather of University of Colorado student Gordie Bailey, who died of alcohol poisoning.

and 0.26 in a 140-pound (63.5kg) female. Both those BAC readings are well over the legal limit for intoxication.

What Makes 21 the Magical Year?

Certainly, one does not have to be underage to participate in drinking games. Indeed, critics of current drinking laws wonder why 21 has been designated as the magical year when young people are expected suddenly to develop a maturity that enables them to drink responsibly. After all, they contend, there is plenty of evidence showing that adults abuse alcohol as well. According to the National Institutes of Health, more than 17 million American adults suffer from alcoholism. People in their twenties, thirties, forties, and beyond binge or find other ways to abuse alcohol.

Anybody who has attended a party with 21-year-old drinkers may see little difference in how they drink and how 18- or 19-year-old revelers consume alcohol. For example, a variation of Century Club played at many off-campus bars is known as Power

Players compete in a beer pong competition in Atlantic City in 2010. While competitors at this event must be 21, beer pong and other drinking games have become popular with underage drinkers around the country.

What Is Alcohol Poisoning?

Heavy drinkers may stumble, slur their words, laugh hysterically, or do things they later regret—such as have sex or try to drive home. People who binge risk much more. In some cases they suffer from alcohol poisoning, which can be fatal.

The first symptoms of alcohol poisoning are confusion and stupor. The drinker may also vomit and suffer seizures. The drinker's breathing will slow and become irregular; people in the throes of alcohol poisoning may take as few as eight breaths per minute.

The drinker's skin will turn pale and may develop a blue tinge. Body temperature will drop. Finally, the drinker will pass out and the heart will stop beating. Sometimes people who die from alcohol poisoning drown in their own vomit. Alcohol can depress the gag reflex that helps prevent choking. Therefore a binge drinker who has collapsed may vomit repeatedly and choke because of a blocked airway.

Alcohol poisoning occurs because the drinker is consuming alcohol faster than the body can process it. The body rids itself of impurities through the liver, which can process the equivalent of one drink per hour. Therefore, consuming more than one drink per hour gives the body more than it can handle, and binge drinking will overwhelm the liver. With the liver unable to perform its cleansing function, alcohol builds up in the drinker's body—soon leading to organ failure.

Hour. The participants are students who celebrate attainment of their legal drinking ages the moment they turn 21. The student and his or her friends go to a bar at midnight, where the celebrating student attempts to gulp down 21 ounces (620ml) of liquor within an hour. It is a goal that many students fail to reach, given the enormous quantity of alcohol they are required to consume. Unable to make their goals, they become sick well before consuming 21 ounces of liquor. Others substitute gulps of beer for shots of hard liquor.

It is all legal—the student reached the age of 21 at the stroke of midnight—but the game illustrates that just because the student is now an adult in the eyes of the law, he or she may not know how to drink like a responsible adult. At South Dakota State University, Jaime Ries describes his Power Hour: "On my birthday, I had 21 drinks—17 shots and four beers."[22] Karl Steege, the manager of Skinner's Pub, a bar near the South Dakota State campus, says he has seen a lot of Power Hours. "Twenty-first birthdays are supposed to be fun," says Steege. "Ninety percent of the time it ends up being not fun because kids are so sick at the end of the night."[23]

Ruth Engs, a professor of health sciences at Indiana University in Bloomington, Indiana, suggests that 21 is not a magical age—that just because somebody turns 21 does not automatically mean he or she is mature enough to drink. Rather, Engs says, a person who learns to drink responsibly before the age of 21 should be regarded as a lot more mature than a person who commences a Power Hour at the stroke of midnight on his or her twenty-first birthday. "Lowering the drinking age would help send the important message that drinking is, in itself, not evidence of maturity," she says. "Responsible consumption for those who choose to drink is evidence of maturity."[24]

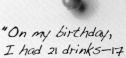

"On my birthday, I had 21 drinks—17 shots and four beers."[22]

— South Dakota State University student Jaime Ries, who played Power Hour on his twenty-first birthday.

Breaking Down Inhibitions

Power Hour players and others who make themselves sick on alcohol consume too many drinks because the alcohol itself has helped cause them to take their drinking too far. Alcohol is a depressant, meaning it slows down the activity in the brain and central nervous system. A person who drinks too much alcohol often makes poor decisions—one of which frequently is to have another drink. Indeed, while they are consuming alcohol, drinkers often find themselves with a false sense of security. They feel emboldened by alcohol and do not realize they are not in control of themselves.

Depressing the activity in the brain has other effects on the human body. When activity in the brain has slowed down, the brain does not do a very good job of communicating with the other body parts. That means the coordination and reflexes of the drinker may be thrown off, which is why intoxicated drivers often cause accidents. The drinker's speech may also be slurred. Emotional responses may be affected as well—that is why some people who drink too much may laugh hysterically and others become sad or sullen.

Also, alcohol often causes inhibitions to break down; that is why the young female drinker would do well to be wary of the boy who insists on refilling her cup. According to statistics compiled by Phoenix House, a New York City–based substance abuse treatment center, 90 percent of rapes on college campuses occur after either the assailant or the victim has consumed alcohol.

Moreover, the center reported, as many as 70 percent of college students who have engaged in sexual activity—both consensually and nonconsensually—admit to having sex with somebody

Caught up in the excitement of the moment, many young drinkers do not realize they are losing control of themselves while playing drinking games. With drinks flowing freely during parties such as this one, they may become disoriented or even pass out.

primarily as a result of being under the influence of alcohol. "Alcohol reduces inhibitions and dulls perceptions so that the woman is less likely to be alert and the man less concerned about what his date wants,"[25] says Andrea Parrot, a Cornell University professor who has studied date rape.

Alcohol and the Adolescent Brain

Alcohol has these effects on people whether they are 18 years old or 38 years old, but there is a major difference between the teenage drinker and a drinker who is much older. Scientific evidence proves that the teenage brain is a work in progress—that the brain continues to develop into early adulthood. Therefore, experts question whether the brain of an adolescent is mature enough to know when he or she has had too much to drink.

The brain is composed of many different parts that throughout childhood, adolescence, and early adulthood are in a continual state of development. During adolescence, one area of the brain still under development is the prefrontal cortex, which is located in the front of the brain just behind the forehead. The prefrontal cortex is responsible for setting priorities, formulating strategies, refining the attention skills of the person, and controlling impulses. "It's the part of the brain that says, 'Is this a good idea? What is the consequence of this action?'"[26] says Frances Jensen, a pediatric neurologist at Children's Hospital in Boston, Massachusetts.

Obviously, drinking can be an impulsive act. If the part of the brain that controls impulsive acts is not fully developed, then there may be no warning signals going off in the drinker's brain to tell the drinker that bingeing is wrong. Says one study written by researchers at the universities of California and Wisconsin: "Adolescents who are high risk takers are more likely to use alcohol, more likely to drive drunk, and more likely to overestimate the prevalence of drunk driving among peers. This suggests that they would be more accepting of risky drinking behavior."[27]

In many cases the adult who drinks too much will wake up the next morning full of guilt and remorse. The adult drinker may resolve never to do it again. If the adult goes on to binge again, it

"Alcohol reduces inhibitions and dulls perceptions so that the woman is less likely to be alert and the man less concerned about what his date wants."[25]

— Andrea Parrot, a Cornell University professor who has studied date rape.

Teenage Drinking and White Matter

A 2009 study by the University of California–San Diego found that binge drinking by teenagers helps destroy the white matter in their brains, which could impair their memories and affect school performance. "We were somewhat surprised that these adolescents who had histories of binge drinking showed significantly poorer quality of their white matter," said Susan F. Tapert, an associate professor of psychology at the school.

White matter is composed of the parts of nerve cells known as axons, which relay messages within the brain. Throughout adolescence, white matter continues to develop, giving young people the ability for recall, which is important for academic performance. By performing magnetic resonance imaging tests on the brains of teenagers, the researchers found a deterioration in the white matter of frequent binge drinkers.

The study suggested that regular binge drinkers have 90 percent of the recall power of young people who do not drink. "If you start drinking in adolescence, you are more likely to go downhill on . . . measures of thinking and information processing," Tapert said.

Quoted in Steven Reinberg, "Binge Drinking May Damage Teens' Brains," *U.S. News & World Report,* April 22, 2009. http://health.usnews.com.

is probably a sign that the drinker suffers from alcoholism and is in need of counseling and rehabilitation. However, most teenagers who wake up the next morning after a night of binge drinking are not likely to believe they did anything wrong. They may look forward to getting to school so they can boast about their drinking experiences to their friends. Chances are, they are looking forward to their next bingeing episode. "It's kind of a bragging thing," says Wyatt Frei, a senior at Tamalpais Union High School in California. "It's considered cool."[28]

Peer Pressure and Rebellion

The desire to brag about a bingeing episode is only one of several motivations that could prompt a teenager to drink. Among the other factors that lead young people toward alcohol are stress, boredom, depression, and rebelliousness. These factors tend to be more of an influence on very young drinkers—those below the age of 18—rather than on college-age drinkers. "Purchasing alcohol illegally is like getting away with something,"[29] says John Doyle, a spokesperson for the American Beverage Institute, a trade association that represents restaurant owners.

Kelsey Bennett says there was an aura of rebellion surrounding her first drinking experience. When she was 13 years old, Bennett invited some friends home. Her parents were not home at the time. Soon, the idea of raiding the liquor cabinet was raised. So Bennett and her friends opened some bottles and poured themselves drinks. "When you start drinking, it's kind of a mystery, something you can't do,"[30] says Bennett, who has gone on to enroll in the Berklee College of Music in Boston.

Peer pressure is also an influential force among young people. Opponents of lowering the drinking age argue that if alcohol becomes more available to young people, more young people would feel pressured by their friends to start drinking. In a study by the University of Pennsylvania, 57 percent of young people between the ages of 14 and 22 said the most popular students are the ones who are most likely to drink alcohol. "The issue is peer pressure," says Larry Handerhan, a senior at Wellesley High School in Massachusetts. "Not from people saying, 'Oh, come on, have a couple of beers,' but from freshmen looking to the seniors as role models."[31] Handerhan's classmate Alexi Wagner estimates that some 90 percent of the students at Wellesley High School have consumed alcohol. "It's an icebreaker," she says, "a stress reliever. Some kids are really uptight and know they don't express their feelings well. If they have a couple of beers, they feel like it's an excuse to let out what they feel."[32]

The University of Pennsylvania study found that other risky behaviors, such as smoking and drug use, are regarded by young people as less likely to be common among popular students, but

> "It's an icebreaker, a stress reliever. Some kids are really uptight and know they don't express their feelings well. If they have a couple of beers, they feel like it's an excuse to let out what they feel."[32]
>
> — Alexi Wagner, Wellesley High School student.

alcohol use is widely regarded as a behavior young people admire. "When you associate behavior with popularity, it makes [drinking] more desirable,"[33] says Kathleen Hall Jamieson, director of the school's Annenberg Public Policy Center, which conducted the study.

Young, Hip, and Sexy

Even when young people sit at home, away from the influences of their friends, they can still feel pressure to start drinking. Simply by turning on the TV or flipping through the pages of a magazine, teenagers can find themselves inundated by images of young, carefree, and attractive people enjoying all manner of alcoholic beverages. Opponents of lowering the drinking age point to the influences of the advertising media on young people: beer, wine, and liquor commercials on TV present drinking as part of a hip lifestyle that many young people find enticing. Says the California-Wisconsin study:

> Given the tendency for viewers to accept what they see on television as normative behavior, the portrayals of drinking and risky physical activities in some beer advertising may make it seem to viewers like these two things are associated in real life. . . . Although viewers of these ads might well know that certain activities, such as snowboarding or jet-skiing, are unwise to mix with alcohol, seeing both appear in the same ad might result in viewers who are more likely to condone risky drinking behavior.[34]

Experts are particularly concerned about the impact of these images on teenage girls, who may be led to believe that they need to drink to be sexy and attractive to boys. Indeed, one recent advertising campaign aired by the tequila distiller Cuervo advised female customers, "Bad girls make good company."[35] Says Susan Foster, vice president of policy research and analysis at the National Center on Addiction and Substance Abuse at Columbia University: "Targeting women is nothing new. The alcohol industry, just like the tobacco industry, knows that if you want a lifetime heavy drinker, the best way is to start them early."[36]

The influence of the media goes beyond TV advertising. A Georgetown University study looked at the advertising content of many popular magazines, including *Vogue, Cosmopolitan, Maxim*, and *Sports Illustrated*, and found an abundance of advertising for alcoholic beverages. The study concluded that people under the age of 18 are exposed to more alcohol advertising than people who are legally permitted to drink. "I don't think it is considered unlady-like to drink a lot," says Ashley, a recent high school graduate interviewed by the *Christian Science Monitor*. "Look at college girls. They are always depicted in the media as getting trashed and they look cool."[37]

The Tragedy of Intoxicated Teen Drivers

While the effects of the advertising media on adolescent minds may be just coming to light, experts have known for decades that the highways are much safer without teenage drinkers behind the wheels of their cars. According to the National Highway Traffic Safety Administration, 28 percent of drivers under the age of 21 who lost their lives in fatal accidents drove while intoxicated. Moreover, the agency says, young drivers who drink are less likely to use their seat belts. The National Highway Traffic Safety Administration says some 74 percent of young intoxicated drivers who died in car accidents were not wearing their seat belts—a safety measure that might have helped save their lives.

"Targeting women is nothing new. The alcohol industry, just like the tobacco industry, knows that if you want a lifetime heavy drinker, the best way is to start them early."[36]

— Susan Foster, vice president of policy research and analysis at the National Center on Addiction and Substance Abuse at Columbia University.

A typical and tragic example of what happens when young people drink and drive can be found in the deaths of Dillon Benavides, 16; his girlfriend, Alex Dicky, 15; and his brother Gus Benavides, 18. The three Bryan, Texas, teenagers were furnished alcohol at a party in August 2008. They left the party after 3:00 A.M. Dillon, who was driving the car, slammed the vehicle into a tree, where it erupted in flames. The bodies of the three teenagers were burned so severely that police had to wait several days before making identifications of the bodies through DNA and dental records.

Later, a lab analysis showed the alcohol content of Dillon's blood at 0.12 percent—well over the legal limit. Meanwhile, after the fire was extinguished, police found a beer keg in the back of the Benavides car. "Every one of them starts out with, 'It's no big deal,'" says Texas Alcoholic Beverage Commission sergeant Randy Field, "but this triple fatality started out with somebody saying, 'This isn't going to be a big deal, buying this keg for them.'"[38]

A short time after the accident, police arrested two 21-year-old men who attended the party: Alex's brother, Wayne Dicky II, and Jimmy Luis Noey. Noey eventually pleaded guilty to supplying the three teenagers with alcohol and was sentenced to a year in prison. Wayne Dicky pleaded guilty to furnishing alcohol to another partygoer who was not involved in the crash; he was sentenced to 45 days in prison.

During the investigation into the crash, police learned that Wayne Dicky was racing the car driven by Dillon Benavides when the vehicle containing the brothers and Wayne's sister struck the tree. A police officer reported that his cruiser was forced off the road by the drag race. He turned his car around and gave chase, but arrived too late to prevent the accident. The police officer reported that Dillon's car actually went airborne before striking the tree. "Wayne spent 45 days alone in jail as punishment for what he did," says Dicky's attorney, Lane Thibodeaux. "I feel confident that he spent every day of that time thinking of Gus, Dillon and the sister he still loves, Alex."[39]

Evidence Abundant and Indisputable

Peer pressure may have a lot to do with why young people like Dillon Benavides and Gordie Bailey drink to excess, then endanger their lives and the lives of others. Bailey and Benavides both attended parties where alcohol flowed freely and others their age drank to excess. Clearly, the Benavides and Bailey cases are examples that give fuel to the argument that most young people are not mature enough to drink responsibly. Indeed, scientific evidence shows that their brains have not yet developed to the point that they can make mature and rational decisions, while emotionally, they may reach for alcohol to help relieve the stresses they feel as teenagers. For all these reasons and others, opponents of lowering the drinking age believe the evidence for keeping the legal drinking age at 21 is both abundant and indisputable.

Facts

- A 2009 University of Michigan study reported that 80 percent of tenth-grade students believe alcohol is either "fairly easy" or "very easy" to obtain.

- According to the Rochester, Minnesota–based Mayo Clinic, such well-known "cures" as black coffee and a cold shower have no effect on ridding the body of alcohol.

- Women get drunk faster than men because their bodies produce smaller amounts of a chemical that slows the release of alcohol in their stomachs.

- Twenty percent of sexually active college students say they fail to use contraceptives when they are drunk, according to Phoenix House, a New York City substance abuse treatment program.

- Power Hour celebrations have resulted in deaths due to alcohol poisoning in California, Michigan, New Mexico, North Dakota, Rhode Island, and Texas, according to the *New York Times*.

- Sixty percent of female college students who contract sexually transmitted diseases report that they were under the influence of alcohol at the time they had intercourse with the infected person.

- A study of the Tamalpais School District in California found that 18 percent of the district's ninth-grade students had binged on alcohol; by the eleventh grade, the number of bingers at Tamalpais more than doubled.

CHAPTER THREE

Can a Lower Drinking Age Reduce Binge Drinking?

While it may seem as though the arguments in support of keeping the drinking age at 21 are difficult to counter, there is, nevertheless, a significant and growing sector of the community that believes the drinking age should be lowered to 18 or 19. And those who are making their case are led by a group of more than 130 college presidents who signed the Amethyst Initiative, asserting that a minimum legal drinking age of 21 is unenforceable and has failed to stem underage drinking and alcohol abuse.

Indeed, the statistics suggest that underage drinking has reached staggering proportions in America. According to the Substance Abuse and Mental Health Services Administration, some 11 million people between the ages of 12 and 20 are believed to drink alcohol every month—that is nearly a third of Americans in the 12 to 20 age group. Of those 11 million drinkers, more than 7 million admit to being binge drinkers. Meanwhile, a University of Michigan study reports that at least 75 percent of American young people have consumed alcohol at least once before they finish high school. The college presidents who signed the Amethyst Initiative believe those statistics provide evidence that the current drinking laws are not only ineffective but have promoted dangerous drinking habits by young people.

The text of the Amethyst Initiative states:

A culture of dangerous, clandestine "binge-drinking"—often conducted off campus—has developed.

Alcohol education that mandates abstinence as the only legal option has not resulted in significant constructive behavioral change among our students.

Adults under 21 are deemed capable of voting, signing contracts, serving on juries and enlisting in the military, but are told they are not mature enough to have a beer.[40]

Advocates for lowering the legal drinking age compare the current laws to the laws in effect during the era of Prohibition, arguing that minimum age drinking laws are no more effective than the laws that banned alcohol for everyone. "Telling underage drinkers they won't have access to alcohol only increases their motivation to drink," says New School University psychologist Stanton Peele. "[That is] why the American prohibitionist model of alcohol education and control for young people is doomed to fail."[41]

"*Adults under 21 are deemed capable of voting, signing contracts, serving on juries and enlisting in the military, but are told they are not mature enough to have a beer.*"[40]

— Statement by the signers of the Amethyst Initiative.

Teaching Responsible Drinking

John McCardell, the former Middlebury College president who organized the Amethyst Initiative, says he became convinced the current drinking laws are ineffective after watching binge drinking and other abusive behaviors grow into epidemic proportions on university campuses. Says McCardell: "If you assume, and I think you have to assume, that alcohol is a reality in the lives of 18-, 19- and 20-year-olds, then you've got two choices. You can try to change the reality. We've been trying to do that and haven't been that successful. That leaves creating the safest possible environment for the reality and there's plenty of evidence to support that 21 doesn't do that."[42]

Following the signing of the Amethyst Initiative, McCardell founded Choose Responsibility, a Washington-based advocacy group that supports lowering the drinking age to 18. The nation's

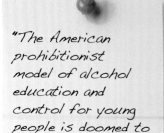

leading voice for lowering the legal drinking age, Choose Responsibility urges high schools to change their "Just Say No" anti-drinking classes into courses that instruct students how to drink responsibly. Under the Choose Responsibility plan, upon completion of the course and passing an examination (and reaching the age of 18), the student would be awarded a "license" that would have to be exhibited in order for the student to be served alcohol. Young people under the age of 21 who do not take or pass the course would still be barred from purchasing and consuming alcohol.

Acting as Adults

The college presidents who signed the Amethyst Initiative cite a variety of reasons for their support for lowering the drinking age. L. Baird Tipson, president of Washington College in Maryland, says he believes it is hypocritical to expect people who are of college age to act in all respects as adults—and yet permit none of them legally to engage in the adult activity of enjoying an alcoholic beverage. He says: "How often has a family with children between 18 and 21 found itself in a restaurant where wine or beer is served with dinner? The awkwardness of asking those children to drink sparkling water while the others share alcohol—in effect creating an artificial boundary between them and the adults . . . emphasizes the unnaturalness of our present laws."[43]

William Durden, president of Dickinson College in Pennsylvania, points out that American colleges have long served as the nation's most important research institutions. Why not devote those campuses and their resources to involvement in a large-scale social experiment: to test whether 18-year-olds are mature enough to drink responsibly. Durden says:

I would like the Dickinson College community—students, parents, faculty and staff and alumni—to be part of a collective effort to reexamine, using all the intellectual and research capacities of higher education in the United States, an issue that truly matters for our society. . . . That issue is the national drinking age and the extreme abuse of alcohol associated with it. Our collective reexamination of this issue through public debate contributes directly to the role that American colleges and universities can play in serving the public interest.[44]

And Lawrence Schall, president of Oglethorpe University in Georgia, says he signed the initiative because he simply came to the conclusion that the current drinking laws are ineffective and change is needed. "As my mother taught me, the sign of either stupidity or stubbornness is to keep doing the same thing in the face of failure," he says. "I see the effects of [alcohol] abuse every day, in automobile accidents, in sexual behavior, in acts of vandalism and assault, in academic performance. I know I don't have the answers, but I also know that the status quo has failed."[45]

In response, opponents of a lower drinking age say they are troubled that some of the nation's leading educators are willing to

Keg parties, such as this one, are a common feature of college life. Signers of the Amethyst Initiative, which seeks to lower the drinking age to 18, believe this action would lead to more responsible drinking habits among college-age students.

put alcohol in the hands of young people. Says MADD president Laura Dean-Mooney, "Parents should think twice before sending their teens to these colleges or any others that have waved the white flag on underage drinking and binge drinking policies."[46]

Pre-gaming in Gainesville

Critics of current drinking laws point out that colleges that have adopted "no tolerance" policies toward underage drinking have been unable to staunch the flow of alcohol. For example, after assuming the presidency of the University of Florida in 2004, J. Bernard Machen was determined to change the college's reputation as a party school. Machen joined the Florida administration after serving as an administrator at the University of Utah, a conservative school where underage drinking is less prevalent. After arriving at Florida's Gainesville campus, he found a well-entrenched party culture. Indeed, during his first two years as president of the university, six students died in alcohol-related incidents. (One died of alcohol poisoning, two in falls, two in traffic accidents, and one in an alcohol-fueled fistfight.)

Machen met with the families of the deceased students and found himself deeply troubled by the deaths. He said he saw how alcohol had shortened the lives of six promising young students, and he vowed to reduce drinking on campus. He initiated a program that requires freshmen to undergo alcohol education courses. He also banned alcohol commercials during the TV broadcasts of Florida athletic events and ordered posters plastered across the Gainesville campus warning female students that heavy drinking often precedes date rape. Says Machen, "A lot of [college] presidents are counseled against doing this because of the negative interactions you have with the student body, but we thought we had to."[47]

Despite Machen's anti-drinking campaign, binge drinking on the Florida campus continues. One of the more troubling trends in alcoholic consumption at Florida and other places has been the tendency to "pre-game"—students begin drinking hours before football games or other large campus events. Once they arrive at the game, the binge drinking continues. When a *New*

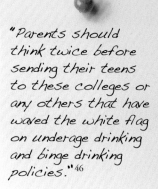

"Parents should think twice before sending their teens to these colleges or any others that have waved the white flag on underage drinking and binge drinking policies."[46]

— Laura Dean-Mooney, president of Mothers Against Drunk Driving.

Are Zero Tolerance Policies Effective?

Ohio University decided to crack down on drinking on campus, so the school adopted a zero tolerance policy. The policy was so tough that students faced disciplinary action even if an *empty* beer can was found in a dormitory room. In the first year following adoption of the policy, nearly 7 percent of the 16,000-member student body was disciplined for violations of the school's alcohol policy. The result? A subsequent study indicated that bingeing by Ohio University students increased 60 percent after the zero tolerance policy was adopted.

Other schools that adopted zero tolerance policies have seen similar results. Indiana University professor Russell Skiba conducted a study of such policies and concluded they do not work. "Zero tolerance is a political response, not an educationally sound solution," he says. "It sounds impressive to say we're taking a tough stand against misbehavior, but the data say it simply hasn't been effective in improving student behavior or ensuring school safety."

Quoted in Join Together, "Report: Zero Tolerance No Solution for Schools," May 17, 2001. www. jointogether.org.

York Times reporter attended a football game at the University of Florida, he found binge drinking already under way on fraternity row hours before kickoff. "We take care of each other," a clearly drunk 19-year-old freshman named Max told the reporter. "We will not let anyone drink under the influence. . . . I mean, drive under the influence. I'm sorry. I'm drunk already. It's been a long morning."[48]

Would Drinking in a Bar Be Safer?

If an intoxicated person such as Max had walked into a bar and asked to be served a drink, the bartender probably would have refused. Most states have adopted laws that prohibit the sale of alcohol to intoxicated persons. Moreover, the intoxicated person would probably have been asked to leave. And if the drunk became loud, abusive, or belligerent—as many people do when they are under the influence of alcohol—a barroom bouncer would be expected to step in and take control.

The signers of the Amethyst Initiative and other advocates argue that lowering the drinking age would help cut down on binge drinking and other abuses. They contend that if students and others are able to drink legally in bars or order drinks with their dinner in restaurants, they would find they have to drink responsibly or they would not be served. Says a statement by the National Youth Rights Association, a Washington-based advocacy group for young people: "Many young people learn drinking in unsafe environments, like basement keg parties. They use alcohol with the intention of getting drunk rather than as an accompaniment to food."[49]

Kathleen Quartaro believes her daughter, Ali, would have been a responsible drinker if she had been permitted to drink legally in a bar or restaurant. Ali, an 18-year-old student at the University of Wisconsin–Milwaukee, died at an off-campus party after a night of binge drinking. After consuming several shots of hard liquor, Ali collapsed and died of alcohol poisoning. Says Quartaro:

> Shortly after learning of her death, in my despair, I grabbed my 17-year-old son and said, "Whatever happened to going out and having a good time with a few beers?" My son's response was: "Mom, don't you think Ali would have loved to go out for a few beers? You can't get beer. Right now it would be easier for me to go out and get some heroin than it would be for me to get beer. And if you could get it you can't be seen with it." That was the moment I recognized that we have a very serious problem in this country. . . . Why are young adults being forced to drink in secret, in environments that encourage reckless, irresponsible behavior?[50]

"We take care of each other. We will not let anyone drink under the influence. . . . I mean, drive under the influence. I'm sorry. I'm drunk already. It's been a long morning."[48]

— Max, a 19-year-old fraternity member at the University of Florida.

Evidence Is Not Concrete

Advocates for lowering the drinking age wonder why young drinkers are forced to hide and yet young smokers are not. They point out that states permit 18-year-old citizens to buy cigarettes, even though diseases attributed to smoking—mostly lung cancer—cost more than 260,000 American lives a year. (And smokers are just not endangering themselves—according to the Centers for Disease Control and Prevention, secondhand smoke is estimated to kill more than 40,000 people a year, mostly due to heart disease.)

Moreover, a report by Choose Responsibility points out that guns are certainly dangerous in the wrong hands, yet many states issue hunting licenses to hunters as young as 12. And, borrowing from the original argument that helped lower the drinking age in the 1970s, Choose Responsibility makes the point that 18-year-old American citizens are old enough to volunteer for active duty in the military yet not old enough to drink. "For better or worse, American society has determined that upon turning 18 teenagers become adults," says the Choose Responsibility report. "This means they can enlist, serve, fight and potentially die for their country . . . but strangely, at 18, [they] cannot buy a beer."[51]

Advocates for lowering the drinking age continually find themselves confronted with statistics regarding the relationship between underage drinking and traffic fatalities. The National Highway Traffic Safety Administration's statistic reporting that 25,000 lives have been saved by raising the legal drinking age is often cited as evidence for leaving the drinking age of 21 intact. According to Choose Responsibility, though, not all of those cases can be attributed to the elevated drinking age. The report points out that since 1974, cars have been much better engineered, making them safer. For example, back in the 1970s air bags were found in few cars, but today they are standard equipment.

During the past few decades, states have enacted mandatory seat belt laws. Back when the drinking age in many states was 18, the report says, seat belt use was generally optional. Overall, the report says, more than 200,000 lives have been saved because of improved safety features in cars—and undoubtedly, in many of

Alcohol 101

Many incoming college students know they face freshman English and math, but now many are learning they also have to sit through "Alcohol 101" courses. Many colleges aim to educate students about the dangers of bingeing and are finding that coursework may be the answer.

About 450 colleges employ the AlcoholEdu online course. All incoming freshmen at those schools must take the course, which lasts for three hours. At the end of the three-hour session, a test is given. AlcoholEdu instructs students about the dangers of bingeing. It also helps students recognize alcohol abuse among their roommates and friends. A University of Illinois study found that students who complete the AlcoholEdu course experience half the alcohol-related problems of students who do not take the course.

A main purpose of AlcoholEdu is to examine common myths students harbor about drinking. Says Nancy Carriuolo, president of Rhode Island College, "The theory is that students commonly overestimate how much their peers consume. If students have more accurate information, they will not feel pressure to drink. AlcoholEdu is a campaign of knowledge that seeks to debunk myths and educate students to the realities of alcohol on campus."

Nancy Carriuolo, "Rhode Island College's New Alcohol Prevention Program—AlcoholEdu for College," April 19, 2007. www.ribghe.org.

those cases the improved safety of the cars helped save the lives of intoxicated drivers, their passengers, and others on the road. "It is clear then that the 21 minimum legal drinking age did not act alone to reduce fatalities (alcohol-related or otherwise) that occurred in the latter years of the 20th century,"[52] says the Choose Responsibility report.

International Trends

Choose Responsibility also points out that the decline in alcohol-related fatalities in America reflects an international trend—that many other countries also saw their highway death rates reduced. Between 1982 and 1992, the report says, the United States experienced a 26 percent decline in traffic fatalities. During the same period, Great Britain experienced a 50 percent decline, while Germany saw its traffic fatality rate fall by 37 percent. The decline in Australia was 32 percent, while in the Netherlands and Canada, each country saw its highway death rate decline by 28 percent. However, the report says, Great Britain, Germany, Australia, the Netherlands, and Canada all have minimum legal drinking ages below 21—and all had steeper declines than the United States in their highway death rates. Says the report, "This downward trend in drunk driving across the industrialized world shows quite clearly that the 21 [minimum legal drinking age] in the United States was, at best, the least effective measure to limit drunk driving amongst these developed countries."[53]

Choose Responsibility believes the drop in traffic fatality rates is due to better safety engineering in cars as well as better driver education, particularly in educating people about drinking and driving. For example, the campaign to select a designated driver—a partygoer who does not drink and takes the responsibility for driving friends home—has been successful in saving many lives not only in America but in other countries as well.

Moreover, many researchers believe that underage drinkers are not necessarily the cause of traffic accidents. Rather, they suggest *inexperienced* drinkers are of much more concern. Therefore, if young people truly do wait until they are 21 to begin drinking, they may find themselves a bit older but nevertheless drinking irresponsibly. A 2001 study by economists Thomas S. Dee and William N. Evans showed that traffic fatalities among young drivers generally peak around age 18, at about 30 per 100,000 drivers, then decline a bit before shooting up again at age 21 to about 28 per 100,000 drivers.

"I remember college campuses when we had 18-year-old drinking ages, and I honestly believe we've made some progress."[55]

— Donna Shalala, president of the University of Miami and a former secretary of the U.S. Department of Health and Human Services.

Police officers stop cars at a busy highway interchange in North Carolina to check for intoxicated drivers. The highway roadblocks, similar to those conducted in many states, are part of an effort to reduce drunken driving.

"Delaying alcohol availability delays the fatalities associated with drunk driving," write Dee and Evans. "This evidence implies that the nationwide increases in the minimum legal drinking age may have merely shifted some of the fatality risks from teens to young adults."[54]

Bingeing Is Socially Desirable

Despite those arguments, many college presidents have decided they cannot support the Amethyst Initiative. Donna Shalala, president of the University of Miami and a former secretary of the U.S. Department of Health and Human Services, declined to add her signature to the statement. She says, "I remember college campuses when we had 18-year-old drinking ages, and I honestly believe we've made some progress."[55]

At the University of Florida, Machen has also refused to accept the position that a lower drinking age would help cut down on binge drinking and has declined to sign the Amethyst Initiative. Writing in the *Tampa Bay Times* newspaper, Machen and Patricia Telles-Irvin, vice president of student affairs at the school, assert, "We do not believe that lowering the drinking age would help solve the largest public health and safety problem here and at other campuses: high risk or binge drinking."[56]

Contrary to the assertions of advocates like Choose Responsibility, Quartaro, and the signers of the Amethyst Initiative, Machen and Telles-Irvin contend that at many colleges, binge drinking is not carried on in secret but is done very much in the open at parties attended by dozens of students. It has become socially desirable for college students to binge on alcohol, Machen and Telles-Irvin suggest, and they doubt whether college students would stop bingeing simply because they reach an age that enables them to drink legally. Machen and Telles-Irvin write:

> Common sense says that most college students binge drink with their friends or at parties. What's appealing about binge drinking is not its "clandestine" nature but that it's socially desirable. Does anyone really think that if 18-year-olds could buy alcohol, the social passport conferred by heavy drinking would lose its caché? The research also clearly supports the minimum drinking age of 21 as both discouraging binge drinking and reducing its danger.[57]

Ongoing Debate

Would a lower drinking age reduce binge drinking? The signers of the Amethyst Initiative—all presidents of American colleges and universities—think so. They believe that current laws setting the minimum legal drinking age have been largely ineffective and unenforceable. They believe the debate about lowering the drinking age should at least be reopened so that lawmakers can start to consider alternatives to simply banning alcohol consumption by people under the age of 21. Other college presidents—in particular those who have not signed the Amethyst Initiative—believe that students have created a culture of drinking at college and will continue to binge regardless of what the law says. Those officials believe the underage drinking laws should be maintained and that colleges would do well to continue their crackdowns and other programs designed to ensure that alcohol stays legally unavailable to students under the age of 21. Because evidence can be found to support both positions, the debate is likely to continue for some time.

Facts

- Among the signers of the Amethyst Initiative are the presidents of Colgate, Dartmouth, Duke, Johns Hopkins, Syracuse, Tufts, and Ohio State universities.

- A 2007 report by the Substance Abuse and Mental Health Services Administration found that 19 percent of 16- and 17-year-olds binge on alcohol each month. The agency also reported that 35 percent of people between the ages of 18 and 20 binge each month, and 46 percent of people between the ages of 21 and 25 binge on alcohol each month.

- The most dangerous day of the week for college-age drinkers is Saturday, according to the Centers for Disease Control and Prevention. On a typical Saturday, the agency says, 42 college-age drinkers die from alcohol-related causes. The safest day is Tuesday, when just 12 deaths occur.

- To discourage drinking on the University of Florida campus, the school stages alcohol-free Gator Nights on Friday evenings. The events include free films, carnival games, and a free midnight breakfast. About 1,000 students usually attend.

- Nearly 250 colleges—about a quarter of the membership of the National Collegiate Athletic Association—have banned alcohol commercials during sporting events.

Can Other Countries Serve as a Model?

Eric Asimov is one of the top wine critics in America. He writes a weekly column about wine for the *New York Times* and has also published articles about wine in many other publications. He has written books about dining and enjoying wine and hosts a weekly radio show on wine. Each week, thousands of wine connoisseurs turn to Asimov to read and hear what he has to say about a wine's color, texture, value, and taste.

Asimov is also the father of two teenage boys and, like most fathers, is anxious to share his interests with his sons. "I can't help hoping that my sons might share my taste in music and food, books and movies, ball teams and politics," says Asimov. "Why should wine be any different?"[58]

Asimov is well aware of the answer: Wine is different because of its alcohol content. Even so, Asimov and his wife planned to give their sons small sips of wine at the dinner table from time to time so they could slowly introduce them to the joys of the beverage. After all, Asimov says, that is how young people learn to drink in Europe. He says:

> In European wine regions, a new parent might dip a finger in the local [wine] and wipe it lovingly across an infant's lips—"just to give the taste." A child at the family table might have a spoonful of wine added to water, because it says, "You are one of us." A teenager might have a small glass of wine, introducing an adult pleasure in a safe and supervised manner. That is how I imagined it in my house.[59]

Lax Attitudes Toward Drinking

Young people in many European countries and elsewhere are introduced to alcoholic beverages by their parents. Indeed, the governments of many countries in Europe and elsewhere have much more lax attitudes about what constitutes a minimum legal drinking age than the state and federal governments in the United States. In fact, America has one of the highest minimum legal drinking ages in the world. Even in Canada and Mexico—America's closest neighbors—the legal drinking age is under 21. In Mexico people as young as 18 are allowed to buy and consume alcohol. In Canada the laws are set by the provincial governments: All Canadian provinces enacted minimum legal drinking ages of either 18 or 19 during the 1970s, and none have raised their drinking ages since then.

Advocates for lowering the drinking age point to other countries as examples Americans should follow. Says Harvard University psychiatrist George Valliant: "If you are taught to drink in a ceremonial way with food, then the purpose of alcohol is taste and celebration, not inebriation. If you are forbidden to use it until college then you drink to get drunk."[60]

As for the Asimovs, they decided to introduce their teenage sons to wine. The Asimovs were careful to go slowly and maintain strict supervision of their sons' drinking habits because, as they learned, despite a culture in Europe that is supposed to teach responsible drinking, it appears that many European teenagers have also learned how to binge.

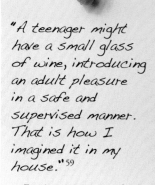

"A teenager might have a small glass of wine, introducing an adult pleasure in a safe and supervised manner. That is how I imagined it in my house."[59]

— Eric Asimov, wine critic for the *New York Times.*

Learning How to Drink

Legal drinking ages vary from country to country in Europe. Germany, Portugal, and Belgium have established 16 as their minimum legal drinking age. Some countries have even lower drinking ages. In Greece it is 14. In England the legal drinking age is 5, although one must be 18 to purchase alcohol. The Netherlands, Slovakia, Hungary, Italy, and Romania have not established minimum legal drinking ages.

In many European countries drinking is part of the culture, and one learns about it at the family dinner table. Wine is viewed as an accompaniment to a meal rather than as a way to get a buzz. Says Southern Methodist University anthropologist Barbara Gallatin Anderson: "To the French, the consumption of wine in quantities of less than a . . . quart is equivalent to abstinence. The mother of a boy of twelve will tell you, though the boy may be sitting across from you with a glass of the diluted wine in his hand, that her son does not drink at all. By this she means that his 'reddened water' contains only a couple of soupspoons of wine."[61] Anderson says she even encountered a French mother who places a few drops of wine into her baby's milk. "In short," Anderson says, "wine drinking is already a habit before French children are old enough to reflect about it."[62]

Young Americans indulge in spring break revelry in the Mexican resort town of Cancun, where the drinking age is 18. Countries around the world have different views on when people should be allowed to consume alcohol.

Family Involvement

The family is also very involved in teaching young people how to drink in Italy and Germany. In Italy young people are taught that wine is part of the meal, and in fact, drinking wine on an empty stomach—which helps speed intoxication—is socially unacceptable. Says University of Turin psychology professor Amedeo Cottino:

> Strong emphasis [is] placed on the consumption of wine in connection with food. This is precisely what is meant by the very common saying, "Never drink wine between meals." This ensures that alcoholic beverages never fill an empty stomach, and it also controls the amount of drinking by relating it to eating times. Moreover, much emphasis is placed upon the negative effects that heavy drinking can have on work and sociability.[63]

Young German boys are also encouraged by their families to learn how to drink. German fathers consider a boy's first beer a rite of passage into adulthood. Often that first beer is consumed at age 16 in the presence of the father and his friends. Indeed, German fathers expect their sons to learn how to drink beer and to learn how much beer will make them drunk so they learn to stop when they have had too much. German girls, on the other hand, are not encouraged to drink, but if they do drink, they are told by their mothers to drink in moderation.

The common denominator in Italy and Germany, as well as in other European countries, is that family members are very much involved in the early drinking episodes of young people, who by and large learn how to drink like their parents. That is not the way most young people learn to drink in America, where most parents ban drinking by the children in their homes. Such bans drive some teenagers into drinking with their friends—as far away as possible from adult supervision. Says State University of New York sociology professor David J. Hanson: "The cultures that are most successful in preventing alcohol abuse are those whose members tend to view alcohol as a natural, normal part of life about which they have no ambivalence. [They] teach their young by example how to drink."[64]

"If you are taught to drink in a ceremonial way with food, then the purpose of alcohol is taste and celebration, not inebriation. If you are forbidden to use it until college then you drink to get drunk."[60]

— Harvard University psychiatrist George Valliant.

Underage Drinking in China

China is the most populous country on the planet, with some 1.3 billion people. About 352 million Chinese are under the age of 18, and according to statistics released by the Chinese government, a lot of them drink.

According to the China Youth Research Center, 80 percent of high school students in China have consumed alcohol. Chinese officials believe the growing economic power of middle-class Chinese citizens has enabled them to afford more luxuries, which means young people there have more spending power. Evidently, young Chinese people are using their new spending power at restaurants, bars, and karaoke parlors that sell alcohol.

In 2006 the Chinese government enacted a ban on alcohol sales to people under the age of 18. Until then, China had no minimum legal drinking age, although many bar proprietors and grocery shop owners refused to sell alcoholic beverages to young people. Under the new law, store owners who sell alcohol to minors can be fined about $250. Said Sun Yunxiao, an official of the China Youth Research Center, "Alcohol abuse among minors has been pretty much ignored in schools and society as compared to drug use or even smoking cigarettes. There has never been an effective mechanism . . . for preventing the problem."

Quoted in *China Daily*, "China Bans Underage Drinking," June 1, 2006. www.chinadaily.com.cn.

Adopting the European Model

Advocates for lowering the legal drinking age in America believe that American families can adopt the drinking culture of the Europeans and teach responsible drinking at home. "The best evidence shows that teaching kids to drink responsibly is better than shutting them off entirely from it," says psychiatrist Paul Steinberg, the former director of counseling at Georgetown University in Washington, D.C. "You want to introduce your kids to it, and get across the point that this is to be enjoyed but not abused."[65]

Ralph Lopez also advocates teaching young people how to drink at home. Lopez, a clinical professor of pediatrics at Weill Cornell Medical College in New York City, started offering his daughter sips of wine at the dinner table when she turned 13. "You have to look at a family and decide where alcohol fits," says Lopez. "If you demonstrate the beauty of wine, just as you would Grandma's special pie, then it augments a meal. However, if there is an issue about drinking within a family then it's a different situation."[66] Certainly, Lopez says, it would not be a good idea for a teenager to start drinking in a home where an older family member suffers from alcoholism.

Opponents do not believe that most American parents would have much interest in teaching their sons and daughters how to drink in moderation. For starters, teaching drinking at home would run counter to the "Just Say No" messages that inundate American households through public service advertising, literature sent home from school, and the constant headlines in the newspapers that detail the tragic consequences of underage drinking and driving. Says Calvina Fay, executive director of the Drug Free America Foundation, "By allowing teens to drink, you are giving permission to your children to do harmful things."[67]

> "If you demonstrate the beauty of wine, just as you would Grandma's special pie, then it augments a meal."[66]
>
> — Ralph Lopez, clinical professor of pediatrics at Weill Cornell Medical College in New York City.

Social Host Laws

Moreover, many states frown on parents who provide alcohol to their children. During the 1970s, as states started raising their minimum legal drinking ages, many left loopholes in place for parents, giving them permission to serve alcoholic beverages to their children at home. Only one state, New Mexico, specifically makes it a crime for a parent to furnish alcohol to a minor.

However, since then many states have seen even those loopholes abused: Parents started serving alcohol at parties for their children and their children's friends. One study by the American Medical Association found that 40 percent of teenage drinkers said they could obtain alcohol from their friends' parents. In response, states started enacting so-called social host laws. These laws hold adults responsible for providing alcohol to underage drinkers when those drinkers go on to commit crimes. In other words, if a person serves alcohol to an underage drinker and that drinker leaves the party and kills somebody in a traffic accident, the adult could face criminal charges.

Social host laws can be particularly strict. In 2002 a Virginia mother and stepfather were charged with serving alcohol to their son and his friends at the boy's sixteenth birthday party. The couple thought they were being careful—they collected everybody's car keys before serving drinks. Still, police learned of the party and arrested the couple. They were convicted and sentenced to eight years in jail—although on appeal a judge later reduced the sentence to five months.

Indeed, many opponents of lowering the drinking age believe that states should toughen their social host laws even further and adopt the New Mexico model, making it illegal for parents everywhere to provide drinks to their children. Says New York University law professor Lis Wiehl: "State laws are simply not strict enough on parents who provide alcohol to minors. Many states allow parents to provide alcohol to their children, and only one state, New Mexico, makes it a felony for any person to knowingly provide alcohol to minors. We need a concerted effort from state lawmakers to close loopholes that allow children to drink on private property."[68]

> "State laws are simply not strict enough on parents who provide alcohol to minors. . . . We need a concerted effort from state lawmakers to close loopholes that allow children to drink on private property."[68]
>
> — New York University law professor Lis Wiehl.

Drinking like Americans

Not only is it unlikely that young Americans will learn how to drink like their counterparts in Europe, but it seems as though the opposite may be happening: Young Europeans are learning how to drink like their counterparts in America. Indeed, the very lax laws and attitudes toward drinking in European countries and elsewhere have led to some of the highest drinking rates in the world. A 2005 U.S. Department of Justice study found that in countries where the minimum legal drinking age is low, rates of consumption of alcohol are typically twice what they are in America.

Why Is It Legal to Drink at Home?

If the minimum drinking age throughout America is 21, why is it legal in most states for parents to serve alcohol to their children? The answer can be found in the U.S. Constitution, which values the privacy of individuals and places strict limits on when authorities can enter the homes of citizens.

Also, states generally assign the enforcement of liquor laws to agencies created to oversee sales and consumption in bars, restaurants, and other businesses. Those authorities have no power over parents—except if they try to buy drinks for their children in restaurants or bars. "We don't have any jurisdiction over what happens in the home," says William Crowley, a spokesperson for the New York State Liquor Authority.

States have enacted social host laws that bar parents from serving alcohol to young people who are not their sons or daughters. And if police or social service agencies learn that parents are giving their children too much alcohol—getting them drunk—they can obtain court orders that permit them to remove the children from the home.

Quoted in Eric Asimov, "Teenage Drinking: Can Sips at Home Prevent Binges?" *New York Times,* March 26, 2008. www.nytimes.com.

For example, the study found that in Belgium, England, and Greece, the typical young person drinks twice as much as the typical American youth. Says the Justice Department report: "Among Americans there is a commonly held perception that American young people drink more frequently and experience more alcohol-related problems than do their European counterparts. . . . [In fact], a great majority of the European countries have higher intoxication rates among young people than the United States."[69]

Choose Responsibility disputes such statistics. The organization agrees that there is more drinking by teenagers going on in

European countries than in America. The organization also cites statistics that show that European young people mostly drink responsibly and there is less bingeing in Europe than in America. Says a Choose Responsibility report, "In southern European countries ratios of all drinking occasions to intoxication occasions were quite low—roughly one in 10—while in the United States, almost half of all drinking occasions involving 15- and 16-year-olds resulted in intoxication."[70]

Still, one young person who admits to abusing alcohol is a British teenager named Lydia, who was interviewed by the British Broadcasting Corporation. Lydia admits that by the age of 16, she was consuming between 2 and 4 quarts (1.9 and 3.8L) of alcoholic cider a night—more than enough to get drunk at each sitting. "I used to go to town and everybody I was with was older than me, and they were all drinking, so I thought, 'Shouldn't I be doing that as well?'" she says. "So I'd start drinking, too. What are you supposed to do?"[71] Lydia finally realized she was doing damage to herself and scaled back—but has not quit drinking entirely. "I drink now in moderation," she says, "and I don't get wasted at every opportunity."[72]

New Crackdowns in Europe

Faced with cases such as Lydia's, European authorities are now looking toward raising their countries' minimum legal drinking ages. A number of public advocacy groups in Great Britain have called on British authorities to raise the legal drinking age to 21. One group, the Institute for Public Policy Research, released statistics showing that 20 percent of English young people between the ages of 11 and 15 drink at least once a week. Says the institute's report:

> In the United States, zero tolerance for drinking and driving and banning those under 21 from drinking anything . . . has reduced alcohol-related accidents by 24 percent since 1982. . . . The [alcohol] industry would no doubt argue that prohibition in the U.S. was hardly a brilliant success [but] can defenders of the status quo credibly argue that the current situation is so perfect that we do not need to at least experiment with alternatives?[73]

Meanwhile, France has already acted—in 2009 the French National Assembly raised the minimum legal drinking age for beer and wine from 16 to 18. (The legal drinking age for distilled spirits was already 18). The French acted after a study indicated the rate of binge drinking among young people in France doubled between 2004 and 2007. Moreover, France has banned alcohol advertising on television and at movie theaters since 1991.

The French government also banned open bars, which are temporary bars set up at sporting events, parades, and similar public gatherings—particularly on college campuses. For small fees, customers can drink as much as they want. Also banned were beer and wine sales at the nation's 13,000 gasoline stations. In France it is believed the gas stations were primary sources of alcohol for young drinkers.

Members of the National Assembly also wanted to ban free wine-tasting parties, which French wine companies sponsor as a way to promote their products. Customers who attend the tasting parties are encouraged to spit out the wine, but government officials suggested that many young people attend the parties simply to drink for free. The proposal failed to get enough votes in the National Assembly to pass, but the fact that French lawmakers looked at banning the events shows how seriously the French government is taking its youth drinking problem.

Pub Crawls in Italy

Italian authorities are also looking closely at changing their laws. In Italy there is no minimum drinking age, although customers must be at least 16 years old to buy alcohol. Italian officials also cite studies that show binge drinking among Italian young people is on the rise. According to Alcoholics Anonymous of Italy, 42 percent of boys and 21 percent of girls under the age of 18 have binged. The Alcoholics Anonymous report said that some 1.5 million Italians between the ages of 11 and 24 are at risk of developing alcoholism. "It's gotten much worse in the last five years," says Gianluca Cecchini, owner of a bar in Rome. "There's a lot more violence, and you see groups of 15 or 20 young teenagers drinking in the streets and causing trouble."[74]

Adds bartender Andrea Codispoti: "They are drinking a lot and they are drinking to get drunk. They don't even like the taste of alcohol, but they feel they need to get smashed to look cool in front of their friends."[75]

The Italians blame young tourists and visiting students from other countries—particularly Great Britain and America—for teaching their teenagers how to binge on alcohol, but there is evidence to suggest the Italians share a measure of the blame. Some Italian entrepreneurs have organized "pub crawls," in which they lead all-night guided tours of some of Rome's hottest bistros. At first, the participants in the pub crawls were visiting American and British students, but now organizers of the pub crawls acknowledge that young Italians are also signing up for the expeditions. Says James Foster, an 18-year-old British citizen who has grown up in Italy: "Being drunk is not as shameful or as embarrassing as it used to be. In fact, it's cool—it's almost to the point

Wineries promote their products at a wine-tasting fair in France. Some French politicians want to ban free wine-tasting parties, which are mainly a venue for people to sample new products but have attracted young people who attend only for the free drinks.

where if you aren't drunk, you're a nobody. Italians are looking to the U.S. and Britain, where it's an accepted thing."[76]

Efforts by the Italian parliament to raise the drinking age to 18 have thus far failed, but local authorities have taken action on their own. In the city of Milan, officials have imposed a fine of about $1,300 on the parents of young intoxicated drinkers. In Rome officials initiated a crackdown on public drunkenness, imposing fines of about $75 on people found drinking on the streets after 9:00 P.M.

A Dying Tradition

Of course, these efforts fall short of the no tolerance policy adopted by all state governments in America, but they do show that authorities in Europe have recognized that young Europeans are no longer drinking as they were taught by their parents. At one time they were taught to savor a glass of wine—to appreciate its taste and how the wine may have made the meal taste better. Evidently, that tradition is on its way to dying out. It seems as though the drinking culture of other countries has, by and large, not served as a model that could be followed by most young Americans. Rather, many young Europeans are adopting the drinking culture of young Americans—often with unfortunate consequences.

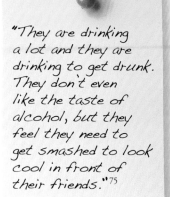

"They are drinking a lot and they are drinking to get drunk. They don't even like the taste of alcohol, but they feel they need to get smashed to look cool in front of their friends."[75]

— Italian bartender Andrea Codispoti.

Facts

• In addition to the United States, the minimum legal drinking age is 21 in just three other countries: Palau, an island nation in the Pacific Ocean, and Mongolia and Indonesia in Asia.

• Per person wine consumption in France is half what it was in the 1970s; however, beer and distilled spirits have replaced wine as the drinks of choice among many French citizens.

- In 1979 the Canadian province of Ontario raised its legal drinking age from 18 to 19; subsequent studies indicated the higher drinking age had no effect on the alcohol habits of young Ontarians.

- The European country with the highest rate of intoxication among under-18 drinkers is the Czech Republic; 61 percent of under-18 drinkers in that country say they get drunk at least once a month.

- The Institute for Public Policy Research study of underage drinking in Great Britain reported that 39 percent of bingers between the ages of 18 and 24 admitted to committing crimes while drunk.

- The French National Assembly has proposed requiring restaurants and bars to employ Breathalyzer tests to detect when patrons have had too much to drink.

CHAPTER FIVE

Do U.S. Lawmakers Favor a Lower Drinking Age?

A dvocates for lowering the drinking age acknowledge that it will not be easy to convince skeptical lawmakers of the need to alter current laws. Indeed, they know it will be quite a challenge to convince state legislators that young adults should enjoy the right to drink alcohol at the age of 18. And even if lawmakers buy that argument, advocates for lowering the drinking age acknowledge that most state governments would still be very hesitant to turn down the federal highway funds that would be withheld should they lower their minimum legal drinking ages.

Turning down tens of millions of dollars in federal highway funds would mean that state lawmakers would have to find ways to finance construction and repair of roads through other sources. Undoubtedly, those other sources would be the local taxpayers. In most places in America, raising taxes so that 18-year-olds may drink legally would not be regarded as a politically popular move. And convincing Congress as well as the president to change the 1984 law withholding highway funds from states is also regarded as an unlikely political accomplishment.

In fact, there does not appear to be much public support for the notion of lowering the drinking age. A 2007 poll by the Gallup Organization reported that nearly 80 percent of Americans oppose lowering the drinking age. Says the pollster, "Americans' attitudes toward drinking alcohol show widespread opposition to lowering the drinking age in all states, and a majority supports making penalties for underage drinking stricter than they are now."[77]

John McCardell shrugs off such statistics. "I have little doubt that I still represent the minority view," says the organizer of the Amethyst Initiative. "But I think the fact that this issue has gotten the attention that it's gotten . . . is evidence in the public's mind that it is not a settled question and that not all the data are on one side."[78]

Little Traction for Lower Drinking Ages

Although polls indicate opposition to permitting teenagers to drink legally, efforts to lower the minimum legal drinking age have emerged in a handful of states. Some of those efforts were prompted by the same arguments made in the early 1970s by the Vietnam era draftees: Young people who volunteer for military duty in Iraq and Afghanistan questioned why they are old enough to fight for their country yet not old enough to drink legally.

Beginning in 2007 state lawmakers in Kentucky, Wisconsin, and South Carolina introduced legislation lowering the drinking age to 18 for military personnel only. None of those proposals found much traction among state government leaders, and all of the bills eventually died. "What do I say to a soldier who comes back from Iraq, having served his country and asks me if he could have a beer?" says Kentucky state representative David Floyd, who sponsored the measure in his state's legislature. "And I just could not possibly imagine myself saying, 'No, son. You're too young.'"[79]

Legislators and advocacy groups in three other states have looked at more sweeping changes in their states' drinking laws, basing their proposals on the arguments made by the Amethyst Initiative. In Missouri advocates hope to slate a ballot initiative that would lower the minimum legal drinking age. However, by 2010 the advocacy group Missouri 18 to Drink had failed to gather the 100,000 signatures required to slate a ballot question. The group's director, Wesley Upchurch, says he is aiming to slate the ballot question in 2012. "Our organization will continue to work hard on this issue," says Upchurch. "Throughout history difficult challenges, such as changing a law, often take

"What do I say to a soldier who comes back from Iraq, having served his country and asks me if he could have a beer? And I just could not possibly imagine myself saying, 'No, son. You're too young.'"[79]

— Kentucky state representative David Floyd.

Cracking Down on Alcopops

Many state governments have taken action in recent years to regulate the sales of so-called alcopops, which are fruity and caffeine-rich alcoholic beverages that critics believe are formulated specifically to appeal to young drinkers. In California, legislators passed a law requiring manufacturers to include wording on the labels that says "Warning: Contains Alcohol." Other states have imposed taxes on the beverages, making them more expensive, which they hope will help keep them out of the hands of young drinkers.

Among the products regarded as alcopops are Mike's Hard Lemonade, Smirnoff Ice, Zima, and Bacardi Breezer. The fruity taste and high caffeine content of the drinks are believed to be particularly appealing to girls, many of whom say the fruit content masks the taste of the alcohol, which many girls find unpleasant.

Critics contend that the alcopops enhance binge drinking because of their caffeine content. Caffeine is a stimulant, which enlivens the drinker's metabolism, making the drinker much more active and therefore more prone to wanting another drink. After several state attorneys general issued complaints, the breweries Anheuser-Busch and MillerCoors agreed to remove the caffeine content from their alcopops. Those products include Tilt, Bud Extra, and Sparks.

several attempts before social and governmental change can occur. Consider our first attempt the beginning of this process."[80]

Meanwhile, in South Dakota, state representative Tim Rounds introduced a bill to lower the drinking age to 19 but found little support for the measure. In early 2010 the bill was killed by a legislative committee whose members worried mostly about losing nearly $20 million in federal highway funds. One of the bill's supporters, state senator Ryan Maher, said binge drinking is a particular problem in South Dakota, where young farmworkers put in long days at work, then binge at night to unwind. "What you have is 19- and 20-year-olds out there drinking unsupervised, driving back roads,"[81] Maher says.

Vermont Willing to Study the Drinking Age

The state where the notion of lowering the drinking age has achieved the most traction is Vermont, where lawmakers have proposed two measures. One would urge Congress to waive the penalties imposed on states for permitting under-21 drinking; the second would establish a commission to study the impact a lower drinking age would have on binge drinking and other forms of alcohol abuse by young drinkers. In 2010 the first measure passed the state senate. Lawmakers next turned their attention to the second measure. "Our laws aren't working," says Vermont state senator Hinda Miller. "They're not preventing underage drinking. What they are doing is putting it outside the public eye. So you have a lot of kids binge drinking. They get sick, they get scared and they get into trouble and they can't call because they know it's illegal."[82]

However, opponents of the legislation soon marshaled their forces. They pointed out that since 1985, when Vermont raised its minimum legal drinking age to 21, alcohol-related traffic fatalities dropped by 40 percent. "I think it is irresponsible legislation, to be quite honest," says William Goggins, director of enforcement for the Vermont Liquor Control Board, which enforces the state's drinking laws. "The facts speak for themselves. Once the drinking age was raised, the number of alcohol-related fatalities decreased. To me, saving lives is the grandest argument of them all."[83]

Elsewhere, opponents of lowering the drinking age say they are prepared to fight it out state by state, if necessary, to maintain minimum legal drinking ages of 21. Indeed, in 2007 MADD, the American Medical Association, and the Insurance Institute for Highway Safety announced formation of a coalition named Why 21? to lobby state legislators to keep the minimum legal drinking

"Our laws aren't working. They're not preventing underage drinking. What they are doing is putting it outside the public eye."[82]

— Vermont state senator Hinda Miller.

67

age at 21. "Science speaks for itself," says MADD spokesperson Glynn Birch. "The 21 law saves lives on the road and keeps countless youths from starting to drink at early ages."[84]

No Federal Cooperation

If advocates in Vermont prevail and win adoption of a lower drinking age, Vermont would stand to lose some $17 million a year in federal highway assistance. Each year, Congress allocates more than $26 billion to highway projects in the states, meaning that if the states lower their drinking ages, they would collectively lose 10 percent of that total, or some $2.6 billion they use to build and repair roads. As one of the smaller states, Vermont would be among those states least affected by the loss. Larger states stand to lose tens of millions of dollars a year. McCardell acknowledges that the 1984 federal law requiring a legal drinking age of 21 for the release of the funds stands as a major roadblock to efforts to lower the drinking age.

McCardell doubts whether there is sufficient support in Congress to adopt an outright repeal of the law but suggests that Congress may be willing—on a case-by-case basis—to grant waivers to states, thus ensuring that they would still receive their full amount of highway funds even if they do lower their drinking ages. To obtain the waivers, he says, states would have to show that they have established the educational and licensing programs proposed by Choose Responsibility. He says, "If Congress would grant a waiver, the states would be willing to try something, and at least then we could get some evidence and see whether things are better or worse."[85]

However, it does not appear likely that the federal government plans to cooperate. Even if majorities in the House and Senate could be convinced to grant the waivers, the legislation would face a veto by President Barack Obama, who is on record as being against relaxing the federal laws that deny highway funding to states that lower their drinking ages.

Moreover, Obama has made it clear that he opposes other measures that would provide access to alcohol to people under the age of 21. For example, he has told members of the military that he favors keeping the drinking age for them at 21. Under

U.S. Department of Defense rules, bars located on military bases must abide by the local laws, which means the legal drinking age on military bases is 21 in all 50 states. (However, the Defense Department does permit members of the military under 21 to drink in other countries as the local laws permit.) During a roundtable discussion with rank-and-file members of the military while campaigning for the presidency in 2008, Obama told them, "I know it drives you nuts, but I'm not going to lower the drinking age."[86]

Cracking Down on Fake IDs

As advocates for lowering the drinking age pursue changes in a handful of states, opponents press for measures that would enhance existing laws, making penalties for underage drinking more severe. A major thrust of their efforts has been to crack down on the use of counterfeit driver's licenses and other forms of fake identification that enable underage drinkers to gain admission to bars or buy alcohol from retailers. Many underage drinkers do not even have to go through the trouble or expense of obtaining fake IDs. They simply borrow a driver's license from an older brother, sister, or friend and find bars where they know that the bartenders and bouncers do not check the IDs too closely.

However, young people caught using fake IDs are finding new and tougher laws with severe consequences. In California a 2008 law increased the fine for trying to buy alcohol with a fake ID from $100 to $250 for the first offense; subsequent offenses could carry fines as high as $1,000. Meanwhile, in Michigan lawmakers increased the maximum penalty for using a fake ID from 30 days in jail to a year in jail. "Using or selling a fake ID isn't a harmless game," says Terri Lynn Land, the secretary of state of Michigan. "It can put the individual and general public at risk."[87] Meanwhile, the federal government has made resources available to state and local governments to help them crack down on fake IDs. In Tucson, Arizona, authorities used federal grant money to buy posters, which have been displayed in all businesses that sell alcohol, warning fake ID users that they could face fines as high as $1,000 if caught with phony cards.

Nevertheless, law enforcement and school officials acknowledge that fake IDs are easy to make; anybody with a high-quality printer and a laminating machine can go into the fake ID business. Indeed, a survey conducted by the Campus Alcohol Abuse Prevention Center at Virginia Tech University found that nearly a third of the school's students admitted to owning fake IDs and using them to gain entry to bars.

Makers of fake IDs charge anywhere from a few dollars to $150 or more for the cards, depending on their quality. "I've heard of people making [fake IDs] on their computers in their dorm rooms," says Meghan Packer, a student at Elon University in North Carolina. "They just didn't really seem too worried, and that's what surprised me was this fearless attitude they had about using them."[88]

In all states, using a fake ID to obtain alcohol is a criminal offense—typically, violators are fined. If the young person is arrested for public drunkenness or driving while intoxicated and police find the person in possession of a fake ID, the penalties can be much harsher. Some may lose their driver's licenses for periods that range from several months to a year. However, unlike an underage drinking charge, young people may be haunted by a fake ID charge long after they leave college. Bruce Phillips, an attorney for Virginia Tech's Student Legal Services, says a future employer who finds an underage drinking charge on a prospective employee's record may be willing to overlook the charge, finding it to be an act of immaturity. However, Phillips says, many future employers are likely to take much dimmer views of job prospects caught using fake IDs. "One of the things about a fake ID charge is that it is considered a crime of moral turpitude," he says. "It is lying, cheating or stealing. It is fraud. That would have more of an effect [on a prospective employer] than an alcohol conviction."[89]

Detecting Homemade IDs

Many bar owners—particularly those whose establishments are located near college campuses—have responded by training employees in the techniques of spotting fake IDs. Employees are

> "I've heard of people making [fake IDs] on their computers in their dorm rooms. They just didn't really seem too worried, and that's what surprised me was this fearless attitude they had about using them."[88]
>
> — Meghan Packer, a student at Elon University in North Carolina.

urged to check the quality of the paper or plastic used to make the ID and to become familiar with the typefaces and photo configurations used on legitimate driver's licenses in their states to help them better detect homemade licenses. Barroom employees may query the ID holders—asking them to provide information on the card, such as middle names. Josh Stevens, the manager of a bar in Blacksburg, Virginia, near the campus of Virginia Tech, says he has quickly become an expert in spotting fake IDs. "I'm not here to ruin people's nights," says Stevens. "I just tell them, 'This is a fake. You have to leave.'"[90]

Critics point out that using a fake ID is not a so-called victimless crime; the true victims in fake ID cases are the bar owners, who face harsh penalties if they ignore IDs or accept obvious fakes. Law

Many bar and liquor store owners use handheld electronic scanners for detecting fake IDs. With the help of a scanner, which reads bar codes and electronic strips on the back of most state driver's licenses, one Indiana liquor store has confiscated dozens of IDs (pictured).

Alcohol at the Movies

A growing trend by movie theaters to sell alcoholic beverages to patrons has raised alarms among government officials, who believe that underage drinkers could find ways to obtain alcohol at the theaters. In Arizona, for example, the state's Department of Liquor Licenses and Control has questioned whether theater staffs have the expertise to recognize fake identification cards or whether enough people are on duty at the crowded concession stands to keep an eye on who is buying the drinks. In response, Scott Cassell, the manager of a theater in Nogales, Arizona, said alcohol would be sold only on nights when patrons have to be 21 to enter the theater. Still, local officials across the country remain skeptical. John Hanson, a member of the city council in Bloomington, Illinois, voted against a proposal to grant a liquor license to a local theater. "The boyfriend is 21 and the girlfriend is 19, and the next thing you know she's already had three drinks underage," he said.

Quoted in Marissa DeCuir, "Some Food and Alcohol with Your Flick? Cinemas Hope So," *USA Today*, March 27, 2008, p. 3-A.

enforcement agencies regularly send youthful-looking undercover officers into bars. These officers carry obvious fake identification cards. If they are able to gain entry to the bar by using the cards, bar owners may find themselves facing arrest and fines totaling thousands of dollars or even loss of their licenses to sell alcohol. Says Jack Keenan, president of the North Wildwood, New Jersey, Tavern Owners Association: "Contrary to what some people might think, we do not want underage kids in our bars. It's illegal, it's dangerous for the kids who attempt it, and it puts our businesses at risk."[91]

In many communities tavern owners have purchased handheld electronic scanners that are capable of detecting fake IDs.

Some cities have even provided grants to bar owners or their trade associations to help them buy the devices. In the resort community of North Wildwood, the city's tavern owners pooled their resources to buy the devices and hired trainers to show them how to use the scanners to spot fake IDs. Moreover, the North Wildwood bar owners said they do much more than simply turn away young people carrying fakes—they confiscate the fake IDs and call the police.

In response, the Amethyst Initiative supporters contend that if it were not for the minimum legal drinking age of 21, there would be no commerce in fake IDs. According to the Amethyst Initiative, the nation's drinking laws prompt teenagers to obtain fake identifications, essentially provoking them into finding other ways to break the law. "By choosing to use fake IDs, students make ethical compromises that erode respect for the law,"[92] the Amethyst Initiative says.

New Blood Alcohol Content Laws

Efforts to toughen the underage drinking laws go beyond the crackdown on fake IDs. In recent years 19 states have lowered the blood alcohol content (BAC) threshold for intoxicated driving from 0.08 to 0.05. Moreover, three states—Minnesota, Montana, and Wisconsin—have lowered the BAC threshold to 0.04. These thresholds apply to drinkers of all ages, but some states have tailored their BAC laws specifically to underage drinkers. For example, in 2007 California lawmakers made it a crime for a person under the age of 21 to drive with a blood alcohol content of 0.01.

Most drinkers would register a BAC of much greater than 0.01 on a Breathalyzer test after consuming a single 12-ounce (354ml) can of beer, 4-ounce (118ml) glass of wine, or mixed drink containing 1 ounce (29.5ml) of hard liquor. Essentially, California has made it illegal for people under 21 to consume more than a taste of alcohol before taking to the road.

The consequences for underage drinking and driving in California are severe—they include loss of a driver's license for up to a year, confiscation of the driver's car, and a fine of $1,000. Actually,

> "Contrary to what some people might think, we do not want underage kids in our bars. It's illegal, it's dangerous for the kids who attempt it, and it puts our businesses at risk."[91]
>
> — Jack Keenan, president of the North Wildwood, New Jersey, Tavern Owners Association.

the fine is the smallest economic consequence of underage drinking and driving in California. According to a study by Stanford University Medical Center in Santa Clara, California, other typical costs of an underage drinking and driving conviction in California include legal fees, $2,500, and the increase in the cost of auto insurance, $6,600. It means the cost of consuming less than a single alcoholic beverage, then getting behind the wheel of a car, could add up to $10,000 or more. Moreover, repeat offenders face even stricter and more expensive consequences.

States such as Massachusetts require repeat drunken drivers to install an ignition interlock device (pictured) in their cars before they can drive again. The driver breathes into the device before starting the car; if a certain level of alcohol is detected on the breath, the device prevents the car from starting.

In addition, young people convicted of underage drinking and driving in California are required by law to list their convictions on their college entrance applications. The law leaves the decision of whether to accept the student up to the schools, but for students who find themselves on the borderline between acceptance and rejection, an underage drinking and driving conviction could provide the college a sufficient reason to reject the applicant.

Ignition Interlock Devices

Other states are taking additional measures to crack down on underage drinking as well as for all people who drive under the influence. For convicted offenders, many states are now requiring installation of ignition interlock devices, which require drivers to breathe into an apparatus that does not permit the car to start if it detects a certain degree of alcohol on the driver's breath. Some states have mandated that the devices be calibrated to react if they detect a BAC of 0.02 on the driver's breath.

The lowering of blood alcohol content levels and the authorization of ignition interlock devices are among the steps that states have taken in recent years to crack down on drinking and driving. Many of those initiatives have been directed at young people in particular to help ensure they do not touch alcohol before their twenty-first birthdays. As the 2007 Gallup poll indicated, support for tougher underage drinking laws is popular among Americans. The politicians who enact those laws have reacted in response to their constituents' demands, making the laws stricter. Indeed, efforts similar to Vermont's willingness to study the issue are rare; rather, most states seem content to maintain their zero tolerance attitudes toward underage drinking.

That means it is likely the minimum legal drinking age in America will remain at 21. And while it is true that many legislators acknowledge underage drinking as a significant problem in their states, most lawmakers do not believe making alcohol legally available to a younger class of drinkers is the way to solve that problem.

Facts

- In 2007 a Virginia high school senior was charged with making and selling more than 100 fake IDs at prices as high as $150 per card; he was convicted and sentenced to 8 months in prison.

- Authorities in Louisiana monitor online social networks, which underage drinkers often use to alert friends about parties. By monitoring Facebook and similar forums, Louisiana officials say they have had widespread success in uncovering underage drinking parties.

- In New Jersey undercover members of the state police infiltrate rock concerts and make arrests when they see young people drinking; at two concerts in 2007, police arrested more than 100 underage drinkers.

- Boys under the age of 21 who drink and drive are 17 times more likely than sober boys to be involved in fatal accidents when their blood alcohol content levels are between 0.05 to 0.08; girls who register that reading are 7 times more likely to be involved in fatal crashes than nondrinking girls.

- A 2008 study found that 28 percent of drivers between the ages of 16 and 20 who were killed in highway crashes had blood alcohol content levels of 0.08 or higher.

- In California, legislation to impose prison sentences on underage drinkers failed to pass the state assembly; sponsors of the legislation said the proposal failed not because legislators felt the penalties would be too harsh, but because they worried California prisons were already overcrowded.

- A 2007 Gallup poll reported that 59 percent of people between the ages of 18 and 34 oppose lowering the drinking age to 18; also, 43 percent of people in that age group favor stricter penalties for underage drinking.

Related Organizations and Web Sites

Centers for Disease Control and Prevention (CDC)
Alcohol and Public Health
4770 Buford Hwy. NE
Mailstop K-67
Atlanta, GA 30341-3717
phone: (800) 232-4636
e-mail: cdcinfo@cdc.gov
Web site: www.cdc.gov

The CDC explores public health issues that affect Americans. By following the link on the agency's Web site to "Alcohol and Public Health," students can find many resources on underage drinking, including videos on binge drinking and so-called alcopops which are caffeinated alcoholic beverages.

Century Council
2345 Crystal Dr., Suite 910
Arlington, VA 22202
phone: (202) 637-0077
Web site: www.centurycouncil.org

The organization was established by American distillers to coordinate efforts by the industry to combat alcohol abuse. The council has made several publications available on its Web site to help curb underage drinking. Publications geared toward teenagers include *Girl Talk* and *Brandon Tells His Story*.

Choose Responsibility

10 E St. SE
Washington, DC 20003
phone: (202) 543-8760
fax: (202) 543-8764
e-mail: info@chooseresponsibility.org
Web site: www.chooseresponsibility.org

Founded by former Middlebury College president John McCardell, Choose Responsibility supports efforts to lower the drinking age. Visitors to the Choose Responsibility Web site can download the report *Debating the Issues*, which provides responses to the statistics and arguments aired by opponents of lowering the drinking age.

Gordie Foundation

2715 Swiss Ave.
Dallas, TX 75204
phone: (214) 823-0235
fax: (214) 823-0236
e-mail: contactus@gordie.org
Web site: www.gordie.org

Established following the death of University of Colorado student Gordie Bailey, the foundation supports efforts to curb binge drinking by young people. Many of the foundation's efforts are aimed toward eliminating the fraternity rituals known as hazing, which in Bailey's case required him to drink a lethal quantity of alcohol.

Mothers Against Drunk Driving (MADD)

511 E. John Carpenter Fwy., Suite 700
Irving, TX 75062
phone: (800) 438-6233
fax: (972) 869-2206
Web site: www.madd.org

Founded by Candace Lightner following the death of her daughter, MADD advocates tougher drunken driving laws, including laws aimed at underage drinkers. By following the link on MADD's Web page for "Statistics," students can find evidence supporting the organization's opposition to lowering the legal drinking age.

National Center on Addiction and Substance Abuse
633 Third Ave., 19th Floor
New York, NY 10017-6706
phone: (212) 841-5200
Web site: www.casacolumbia.org

Sponsored by Columbia University, the center examines the impact of substance abuse on society. By visiting the organization's Web site, students can download several reports on underage drinking, including *Teen Tipplers: America's Underage Drinking Epidemic* and *Rethinking Rites of Passage: Substance Abuse on America's Campuses.*

National Highway Traffic Safety Administration (NHTSA)
1200 New Jersey Ave. SE
West Building
Washington, DC 20590
phone: (888) 327-4236
Web site: www.nhtsa.gov

The NHTSA administers all federally sponsored highway safety programs. Extensive information on underage drinking and driving is available through the site's link to "Impaired Driving."

National Institute on Alcohol Abuse and Alcoholism (NIAAA)
5635 Fishers Ln., MSC 9304
Bethesda, MD 20892-9304
phone: (301) 443-3860
e-mail: niaaaweb-r@exchange.nih.gov
Web site: www.niaaa.nih.gov

An agency of the National Institutes of Health, the NIAAA supports scientific research into alcohol-related issues. A project of the NIAAA is the Alcohol Policy Information System, which explores underage and binge drinking. The project Web site provides an overview of state laws and the text of the 1984 National Minimum Drinking Age Act.

Students Against Destructive Decisions (SADD)

255 Main St.
Marlborough, MA 01752
phone: (877) 723-3462
fax: (508) 481-5759
e-mail: info@sadd.org
Web site: www.sadd.org

Established by Massachusetts high school students in 1981 as Students Against Drunk Driving, SADD has grown into a national organization that helps young people resist peer pressure and other causes of underage drinking, bingeing, and drunken driving. The organization provides facts and statistics relating to drinking and other bad decisions by teenagers.

Substance Abuse and Mental Health Services Administration (SAMHSA)

1 Choke Cherry Rd.
Rockville, MD 20857
phone: (877) 726-4727
fax: (240) 221-4292
Web site: www.samhsa.gov

The federal agency explores trends and motivations behind drinking by young people. Visitors to the SAMHSA Web site can find extensive statistics and discussions about trends in underage drinking by downloading the report *Underage Alcohol Use: Findings from the 2002–2006 National Surveys on Drug Use and Health.*

Additional Reading

Books

George W. Dowdall, *College Drinking: Reframing a Social Problem.* Westport, CT: Praeger, 2008.

David Edvin and Samuel Harald, eds., *Underage Drinking: Examining and Preventing Youth Use of Alcohol.* Hauppauge, NY: Nova Science, 2010.

David N. Jolly, *DUI/DWI: The History of Driving Under the Influence.* Parker, CO: Outskirts, 2009.

Barrett Seaman, *Binge: What Your College Student Won't Tell You.* Hoboken, NJ: Wiley, 2006.

Chris Volkmann and Toren Volkmann, *From Binge to Blackout: A Mother and Son Struggle with Teen Drinking.* New York: New American Library, 2006.

Periodicals

Greg Edmonds, "Center of the Storm," *Roanoke (VA) Times*, June 29, 2009.

John Hechinger, "Bid to Reconsider Drinking Age Taps Unlikely Supporters; College Presidents Say Current Law Leads to More Abuse," *Wall Street Journal*, August 21, 2008.

Judy Keen, "States Weigh Lowering Drinking Age," *USA Today*, March 21, 2008.

Kevin Sack, "At the Legal Limit," *New York Times*, November 2, 2008.

Nick Squires, "Binge Drinking Spreads to Italy," *Christian Science Monitor*, October 11, 2009.

Web Sites

Amethyst Initiative (www.amethystinitiative.org). More than 130 college presidents have signed the Amethyst Initiative, which calls for lowering the drinking age below 21. Students can read the statement signed by the college presidents. A list of who signed the statement is also available, as well as comments from several presidents on why they think the current drinking laws are ineffective.

Mayo Clinic: Alcohol Poisoning (www.mayoclinic.com/health/alcohol-poisoning/DS00861). The world-renowned research hospital in Rochester, Minnesota, provides an overview of alcohol poisoning on its Web site. Visitors can read about the symptoms, risk factors, and complications that stem from binge drinking.

National Commission on Marihuana and Drug Use: History of Alcohol Prohibition (www.druglibrary.org/schaffer/library/studies/nc/nc2a.htm). Visitors can read an extensive history of the drinking laws in America, starting in the 1600s when the first settlers arrived. The Web page also covers the temperance movement, the era of Prohibition, and the Vietnam War era, when many states lowered their drinking ages below 21.

National Youth Rights Association (www.youthrights.org/drinkingage.php). The Washington, D.C.–based lobbying group for the rights of young people has argued in favor of lowering the drinking age. Visitors to the association's Web site can find position papers, research reports, and news articles supporting a lower drinking age.

***Roanoke Times*: Under 21** (roanoke.com/multimedia/under21/main/stories). The staff of the *Roanoke Times* in Virginia has produced an extensive archive of stories covering the drinking age debate. In addition to numerous news articles, the newspaper has also produced a data bank of alcohol-related statistics and several video interviews with experts and students.

Source Notes

Introduction: Reopening the Debate

1. Quoted in Kevin Kittredge, "Parties Pushed Off Campus," *Roanoke (VA) Times*, October 25, 2009, p. A-1.

2. Quoted in Kittredge, "Parties Pushed Off Campus," p. A-1.

3. Quoted in John Hechinger, "Bid to Reconsider Drinking Age Taps Unlikely Supporters; College Presidents Say Current Law Leads to More Abuse," *Wall Street Journal*, August 21, 2008, p. A-3.

4. Quoted in Judy Keen, "States Weigh Lowering Drinking Age," *USA Today*, March 21, 2008, p. A-3.

5. Quoted in Michael Patterson, "Virginia Offers Sobering Consequences to Drinking, Driving," *Washington and Lee Trident*, March 16, 2005. http://media.www.thetrident.org.

Chapter One: What Are the Origins of the Drinking Age Controversy?

6. National Highway Traffic Safety Administration, *Sentencing and Dispositions of Youth DUI and Other Alcohol Offenses: A Guide for Judges and Prosecutors*, 1999. www.nhtsa.gov.

7. Quoted in *60 Minutes*, "The Debate on Lowering the Drinking Age," CBS News, February 22, 2009. www.cbsnews.com.

8. Mark Edward Lender and James Kirby Martin, *Drinking in America: A History*. New York: Free Press, 1987, p. 181.

9. Quoted in David J. Hanson, *Preventing Alcohol Abuse: Alcohol, Culture and Control*. Westport, CT: Greenwood, 1995, p. 10.

10. Lender and Martin, *Drinking in America*, p. 47.

11. Carla T. Main, "Underage Drinking and the Drinking Age," *Policy Review*, June–July 2009, p. 35.

12. George Barton Cutten, "Meet a Prohibitionist," *Vital Speeches of the Day*, October 1, 1939, p. 758.

13. Lender and Martin, *Drinking in America*, p. 180.

14. Quoted in Marc Jason Gilbert, ed., *The Vietnam War on Campus: Other Voices, More Distant Drums*. Westport, CT: Greenwood, 2001, p. 235.

15. Main, "Underage Drinking and the Drinking Age," p. 35.

16. Quoted in *60 Minutes*, "The Debate on Lowering the Drinking Age."

17. Quoted in Nancy Faber, "Clarence Busch, the Drunk Driver Who Inspired a Movement, Faces Prison After Another Accident," *People Weekly*, October 14, 1985. www.people.com.

18. Quoted in James J. Florio, "Raise It to 21 and End the Carnage," *American Bar Association Journal*, April 1984, p. 20.

19. Quoted in Florio, "Raise It to 21 and End the Carnage," p. 20.

20. Florio, "Raise It to 21 and End the Carnage," p. 18.

Chapter Two: Are Teenagers Mature Enough to Drink?

21. Quoted in *60 Minutes*, "The Debate on Lowering the Drinking Age."

22. Quoted in Ruth Brown, "Power Hour Not Only Way to Turn 21," *South Dakota State University Collegian*, March 5, 2008. http://media.www.sdsucollegian.com.

23. Quoted in Brown, "Power Hour Not Only Way to Turn 21."

24. Quoted in Alcohol: Problems and Solutions, "The Drinking Age Should Be Lowered: Interview with Dr. Ruth Engs," 2009. www2.potsdam.edu.

25. Andrea Parrot, *Coping with Date Rape and Acquaintance Rape*. New York: Rosen, 1999, p. 35.

26. Quoted in Richard Knox, "The Teen Brain: It's Just Not Grown Up Yet," National Public Radio, March 1, 2010. www.npr.org.

27. Lara Zwarun, Daniel Linz, Miriam Metzger, and Dale Kunkel, "Effects of Showing Risk in Beer Commercials to Young

Drinkers," *Journal of Broadcasting and Electronic Media*, March 2006, p. 57.

28. Quoted in Jim Staats, "Tamalpais School District Combats Teen Binge Drinking," *Marin Independent Journal*, March 4, 2009. www.marinij.com.

29. Quoted in Hans S. Nichols, "Getting Drunk on Rebellion," *Insight*, July 16, 2001, p. 19.

30. Quoted in Elizabeth Armstrong, Christina McCarroll, and Carly Baldwin, "Behind the Rise in Underage Drinking," *Christian Science Monitor*, July 8, 2004, p. 1.

31. Quoted in Ross Atkin, "Teens Speak Up About Drinking," *Christian Science Monitor*, January 17, 2001, p. 17.

32. Quoted in Atkin, "Teens Speak Up About Drinking," p. 17.

33. Quoted in Karen Thomas, "Kids' Consensus: Popularity Shapes Behavior," *USA Today*, July 2, 2002, p. 9-D.

34. Zwarun et al., "Effects of Showing Risk in Beer Commercials to Young Drinkers," p. 56.

35. Quoted in Armstrong et al., "Behind the Rise in Underage Drinking," p. 1.

36. Quoted in Armstrong et al., "Behind the Rise in Underage Drinking," p. 1.

37. Quoted in Armstrong et al., "Behind the Rise in Underage Drinking," p. 1.

38. Quoted in Cassie Smith, "Two Men Linked to Fiery Wreck," *Bryan-College Station (TX) Eagle*, September 5, 2008. www.theeagle.com.

39. Quoted in Kelly Brown, "Brother of Victim Jailed for 45 Days," *Bryan-College Station (TX) Eagle*, September 25, 2008. www.theeagle.com.

Chapter Three: Can a Lower Drinking Age Reduce Binge Drinking?

40. Amethyst Initiative, "It's Time to Rethink the Drinking Laws," 2010. www.amethystinitiative.org.

41. Stanton Peele, "The Bizarre Effort to Eliminate Underage Drinking in the United States: A Harm Reduction Approach to Youthful Drinking," *Addiction Research and Theory*, June 2007, p. 227.

42. Quoted in Kevin Sack, "At the Legal Limit," *New York Times*, November 2, 2008, p. EL-20.

43. Quoted in Amethyst Initiative, "Why I Signed," 2010. www.amethystinitiative.org.

44. Quoted in Amethyst Initiative, "Why I Signed."

45. Quoted in Amethyst Initiative, "Why I Signed."

46. Quoted in Lini S. Kadaba, "Colleges Get Drinking Debate They Asked For," *Philadelphia Inquirer*, August 20, 2008, B-1.

47. Quoted in Sack, "At the Legal Limit," p. EL-20.

48. Quoted in Sack, "At the Legal Limit," p. EL-20.

49. National Youth Rights Association, "Position Paper: Drinking Age," 2005. www.youthrights.org.

50. Kathleen Quartaro, "Kathleen's Story," Choose Responsibility, 2010. www.chooseresponsibility.org.

51. Choose Responsibility, *Debating the Issues*, 2010. www.amethystinitiative.org.

52. Choose Responsibility, *Debating the Issues*.

53. Choose Responsibility, *Debating the Issues*.

54. Thomas S. Dee and William N. Evans, "Behavioral Policies and Teen Traffic Safety," *American Economic Review*, May 2001, p. 94.

55. Quoted in Justin Pope, "Is It Time to Lower the Drinking Age? Some College Presidents Say Yes," *St. Louis Post-Dispatch*, August 19, 2008, p. A-1.

56. J. Bernard Machen and Patricia Telles-Irvin, "Lowering the Drinking Age: Not the Solution to Binge Drinking," *Tampa Bay Times*, August 25, 2008. www.tampabay.com.

57. Machen and Telles-Irvin, "Lowering the Drinking Age."

Chapter Four: Can Other Countries Serve as a Model?

58. Eric Asimov, "Teenage Drinking: Can Sips at Home Prevent Binges?" *New York Times*, March 26, 2008. www.nytimes.com.

59. Asimov, "Teenage Drinking."

60. Quoted in Asimov, "Teenage Drinking."

61. Quoted in Mac Marshall, ed., *Beliefs, Behaviors and Alcoholic Beverages: A Cross-Cultural Survey*. Ann Arbor: University of Michigan Press, 2000, p. 432.

62. Quoted in Marshall, *Beliefs, Behaviors and Alcoholic Beverages*, p. 432.

63. Quoted in Dwight B. Heath, ed., *International Handbook on Alcohol and Culture*. Westport, CT: Greenwood, 1995, p. 157.

64. Quoted in Heath, *International Handbook on Alcohol and Culture*, pp. 311–12.

65. Quoted in Asimov, "Teenage Drinking."

66. Quoted in Asimov, "Teenage Drinking."

67. Quoted in Jennifer Pifer, "Author: Letting Kids Drink Early Reduces Bingeing," CNN, September 27, 2007. www.cnn.com.

68. Lis Wiehl, "Parents: Underage Drinking Is Illegal, Even Under Your Roof," Fox News, May 29, 2007. www.foxnews.com.

69. U.S. Department of Justice, Office of Juvenile Justice and Delinquency Prevention, *Youth Drinking Rates and Problems: A Comparison of European Countries and the United States*, 2005. www.pire.org.

70. Choose Responsibility, *Debating the Issues.*

71. Quoted in BBC, "I Hope I Haven't Damaged Myself," November 17, 2006. http://newsvote.bbc.co.uk.

72. Quoted in BBC, "I Hope I Haven't Damaged Myself."

73. Jasper Gerard, "Should We Raise the Age of Legal Drinking?" *Public Policy Research*, March–May 2007, p. 34.

74. Quoted in Nick Squires, "Binge Drinking Spreads to Italy," *Christian Science Monitor*, October 11, 2009, p. 12.

75. Quoted in Squires, "Binge Drinking Spreads to Italy."

76. Quoted in Squires, "Binge Drinking Spreads to Italy."

Chapter Five: Do U.S. Lawmakers Favor a Lower Drinking Age?

77. Joseph Carroll, "Most Americans Oppose Lowering Legal Drinking Age to 18 Nationwide," Gallup Organization, July 27, 2007. www.gallup.com.

78. Quoted in Greg Edmonds, "Center of the Storm," *Roanoke (VA) Times*, June 29, 2009, p. A-14.

79. Quoted in WLKY News, "Lawmaker Pre-files Bill Lowering Drinking Age for Military Personnel," December 18, 2007. www.wlky.com.

80. Wesley Upchurch, "Missouri 18 to Drink Ballot Initiative," Facebook, 2010. www.facebook.com.

81. Quoted in Dirk Lammers, "Lawmakers Kill Rounds' Bill to Lower Drinking Age," *Pierre (SD) Capital Journal*, February 22, 2010. www.capjournal.com.

82. Quoted in Associated Press, "Vermont Mulls Lower Drinking Age," *USA Today*, February 29, 2008. www.usatoday.com.

83. Quoted in Associated Press, "Vermont Mulls Lower Drinking Age."

84. Quoted in Jennifer Parker, "Group Stirs Debate on Legal Drinking Age," ABC News, October 9, 2007. http://abcnews.go.com.

85. Quoted in Associated Press, "Vermont Mulls Lower Drinking Age."

86. Quoted in CBS News, "Obama to Army Vet: No Lower Drinking Age," March 17, 2008. www.cbsnews.com.

87. Quoted in Michigan Office of the Secretary of State, "Secretary Land Welcomes Legislation Boosting Penalties for State ID Fraud," news release, June 30, 2004. www.michigan.gov.

88. Quoted in WRAL-TV, "Fake IDs Stoke Underage Drinking Problem," March 9, 2007. www.wral.com.

89. Quoted in Adrian Gomez Licon, "Fake IDs a Real Concern," *Roanoke (VA) Times*, November 3, 2009. www.roanoke.com.

90. Quoted in Licon, "Fake IDs a Real Concern."

91. Quoted in Joe Hart, "North Wildwood Bar Owners Battle Underage Drinking," *Cape May County (NJ) Herald*, May 15, 2009. www.capemaycountyherald.com.

92. Amethyst Initiative, "It's Time to Rethink the Drinking Laws."

Index

Note: Boldface page numbers refer to illustrations.

blood alcohol concentration
(BAC)
 body size/gender as factors in,
  14
 increased risk of car crashes
  and, 24
 threshold for intoxication
  establishment of 0.08
   national standard, 23
  states lowered to 0.05, 0.04,
   or 0.01, 73
brain
 adolescent, alcohol and, 31–32
 effects of alcohol on, 29–31
Breathalyzer testing, 22–23, 63,
 73
Burchett, Adam, 9
Busch, Clarence, 20

California, consequences for
 underage drinking and driving
 in, 73–75
Cassell, Scott, 72
Cecchini, Gianluca, 60
Centers for Disease Control and
 Prevention (CDC), 45, 50
China, underage drinking in, 55
Choose Responsibility, 39–40,
 45, 47, 58–59, 78
Christian Science Monitor, 35
Codispoti, Andrea, 61
Cottino, Amedeo, 54
Crowley, William, 58
Cutten, George Barton, 17

Dean-Mooney, Laura, 42
deaths
 from alcohol-related traffic
  accidents

among youth, 9, 10, 35–36
 international decline in,
  47–48
 annual, of college students from
  alcohol-related causes, 26
Dee, Thomas S., 47–48
Department of Justice, U.S., 57
Dicky, Alex, 35
Dicky, Wayne, II, 36
Doyle, John, 33
drinking age
 lives saved since raising of, 7,
  45
 lowering
  consequences to states from,
   68
  as means to combat binge
   drinking, 38–41
  opposition to, 48–49
 public opinion on, **8**, 64, 76
 state attempts at, 65–68
 in other countries, 52, 62
drinking games, 26–29
driving under the influence
(DUI)
 adolescent
  BAC levels and, 24
  deaths from, 9, 10, 35–36
  increases in state penalties for,
   73–75
  percent of all fatal accidents
   involving, 19
  seat belt use and, 35
 changes in attitudes about,
  12–13
Dunphy, Katie, 6–7
Durden, William, 40

Ehrhart, William D., 18

Picture Credits

Cover: iStockphoto.com

Maury Aaseng: 8

AP Images: 12, 16, 23, 27, 30, 48, 53, 61, 71, 74

Photoshot: 41

About the Author

A former newspaper reporter and columnist, Hal Marcovitz is the author of more than 150 books for young readers. He makes his home in Chalfont, Pennsylvania, with his wife, Gail, and daughter Ashley.